THE FLAG,
THE CROSS, AND THE
STATION WAGON

THE FLAG,
THE CROSS,
AND THE
STATION WAGON

. . . .

A Graying American Looks Back at
His Suburban Boyhood and Wonders
What the Hell Happened

BILL McKIBBEN

HENRY HOLT AND COMPANY   NEW YORK

Henry Holt and Company
Publishers since 1866
120 Broadway
New York, New York 10271
www.henryholt.com

Henry Holt® and ⒽⓉ® are registered trademarks of
Macmillan Publishing Group, LLC.

Library of Congress Cataloging-in-Publication Data is available

ISBN: 9781250823601

Our books may be purchased in bulk for promotional, educational, or
business use. Please contact your local bookseller or the Macmillan Corporate and
Premium Sales Department at (800) 221-7945, extension 5442, or by e-mail at
MacmillanSpecialMarkets@macmillan.com.

First Edition 2022

Designed by Kelly S. Too

Printed in the United States of America

1 3 5 7 9 10 8 6 4 2

For Gordon McKibben (1930–1999) and for Peggy McKibben

CONTENTS

The Setting   1

The Flag   23

The Cross   87

The Station Wagon   147

People of a Certain Age   199

Notes, Sources, and Acknowledgments   219

THE FLAG,
THE CROSS, AND THE
STATION WAGON

THE SETTING

· · · · · · · ·

In my tenth year, in 1970, my family—my mom, my dad, my seven-year-old brother, and I—moved into the American suburbs. More precisely, we moved to the town of Lexington, Massachusetts, a community of thirty thousand people which sat a dozen miles outside Boston. Our home, which cost $30,000, was like a child's drawing of a suburban home: a square block with a door and a window on the ground floor and two windows on the story above, one looking out from my bedroom and the other from Tom's. A single big maple spread its branches over the front lawn and the driveway, dropping leaves on the maroon Plymouth that carried my father on his daily commute. We were as statistically average as it was possible to be, a near-perfect example of the white American middle class then in the process of rocketing to a prosperity—a widespread, shared, suburban standard of living—that the world had never before seen. We lived, and this is the truth, halfway down a leafy road called Middle Street.

So what the hell happened? How did we go from an America where that kind of modest paradise seemed destined to spread to more and more of the country to the doubtful nation we inhabit fifty years later: a society strained by bleak racial and economic inequality, where life expectancy was falling even before a pandemic that deepened our divisions, on a heating planet whose physical future is dangerously in question?

Since the suburb has dominated our landscape over those decades, some of the answers must lie there—and in the generations that grew up there, those of us baby boomers who still weigh so heavily on the political and financial life in the United States. As Ta-Nehisi Coates once wrote, his fears as a young Black man were somehow "connected to the Dream out there, to the unworried boys, to pie and pot roast, to the white fences and green lawns nightly beamed into our television sets." That was my pot roast, and I'm convinced he's right—that you can see some of the roots of what went wrong back in those shady streets of my boyhood. And not only with race, but also with democracy, and with the planet. I'm convinced, in fact, that Lexington, because it was both very typical and slightly set apart by its place in American history, provides an unusually sharp lens through which to view those times, and our time. I'm curious about what went so suddenly sour with American patriotism, American faith, and American prosperity—the flag, the cross, and the station wagon. I'm curious if any of that trinity can, or should, be reclaimed in the fight for a fairer future.

I've never thought my own history was much worth recounting, because it was mostly free of the angst and suffering that have anchored memoirs in recent years. That's why for much of my life I've concentrated on telling the stories of others as best I can. But perhaps that very averageness is the thing that makes my own history a little useful, at least if we're trying to understand what went wrong. This is as much memoir as I'm likely to write, but it's as much the story of a place as of a person.

So let me tell you about two important events that happened in 1971, the year after we arrived in Lexington. I was aware of one of them at the time; the other I learned about only recently. In deference to Dr. Seuss, a literary staple of that era when books were already fighting a rearguard battle against TV, I will call those events Thing One and Thing Two, and they will be touchstones throughout this book. But to understand them, you need to understand the particular town they were set in. And if you didn't live through that time, perhaps this short recounting of one town's history will give you a feel for the truly remarkable rise of suburbia.

LEXINGTON WAS WHERE the American Revolution began in 1775, and we will return to that history throughout this book. But by, say, 1900, its past was past, and its present was largely . . . dairy. The community produced more milk on its small farms than any town in Massachusetts save one. The milk rode the train into Boston each morning—but so, slowly, did more and more residents; as the twentieth century began, Lexington was in the process of turning from a farm town into a bedroom community for the expanding metropolis. From thirty-eight hundred people in 1900, it grew to thirteen thousand by the start of World War II—and then, in the war's aftermath, it took off, more than doubling in size by 1960. Which was exactly what was happening everywhere else—between 1950 and 1970, America's suburban population nearly doubled to seventy-four million, with 83 percent of all the country's growth coming in such places.

One of the few modern histories of Lexington was sponsored, appropriately, by the town's bank, and the introduction to that volume concludes: "As 1946 dawned, the town of Lexington was faced with the challenge of employing and housing returning veterans and educating their children. The great American postwar expansion was about to begin, and with it came the 'baby boom.' Lexington Savings Bank was ready to support this growth with savings accounts and mortgage loans." Savings accounts and mortgage loans will be central preoccupations of this book, but at the time they must have seemed mundane and obvious features of a rapidly multiplying prosperity. By 1949, the local newspaper was reporting on proposed bids for a big new high school; a new four-story wing was under construction at the local hospital where four hundred babies had been born in the previous twelve months; and the town's Board of Selectmen were discussing "the phenomenal expansion" of Lexington in the postwar years, with 947 new permits granted for single-family dwellings. That expansion was just beginning. By 1952 (when Clarabell, the clown from television's *Howdy Doody Show*, made a much-awaited appearance at a local shoe store, and construction began on a "new, ultra-modern" A&P grocery store with "a self-service meat department and automatic doors"), school enrollment had begun to set new records that would continue to be broken each fall for decades.

If there were a few dark shadows—the civil defense agency wanted to blood type all residents "in case of atomic attack," and the town's first air-raid test fizzled when "the fire whistle malfunctioned and sounded for a full ten minutes instead of a series of short bursts"—most of the news from the '50s and early '60s was about progress and growth. Color television had "its first public showing" in 1954 when the local appliance store unveiled the latest Motorola; the Salk vaccine eradicated polio (and without resistance from local residents); a sonic boom, "the first purposeful breaking of the sound barrier in the Greater Boston area," enlivened patriotic observations in 1956. Yes, the town's oldest tree was cut down in 1960, a victim of Dutch elm disease, and yes, odor complaints finally led to the revocation of the license for the town's last remaining piggery, but against that, "the Beatles, an English musical group causing international news," landed at the local airport en route to a Boston concert. And the local garden center reported selling a ton of birdseed every week, even as mosquito control authorities announced their success spraying a miracle agent, DDT, from helicopters over the town's wetlands to control that ancient pest.

As the 1960s wore on, however, even the most bucolic suburbs couldn't escape the tensions starting to roil America. Hanscom Field, the U.S. Air Force base that straddled the town line and where the Beatles touched down, grew noisier as the war in Southeast Asia expanded; the Air Force's Electronic Systems Division was established there to consolidate its electronic systems under one command (the computerized network for detecting incoming ICBM warheads was eventually called the Lexington Discrimination System). More and more local boys were drafted—one wrote in 1965 to say he "would pay $1,000 to be able to lie down at the Lexington Common with a tall glass of iced tea." That same year NBC arrived to film an hour-long special, *The World of the Teenager*. Town pride at being selected for the documentary "turned to anger" when the show aired, local historian Richard Kollen reports—footage of local youth learning to waltz in jacket and tie or long dresses was intercut with scenes from "rock and roll dance parties" and "coffee houses," reflecting what the narrator called "a teenage restlessness, stirring, and doubt. Throughout America there is a widespread dissatisfaction among young people with what has been handed down to them, with adult values and with established tradition." Kids complained to the camera that the town was dull, with nothing for them to do; the police chief insisted that the trouble was "overpermissiveness in the home." One adult explains: "I think this is the period of the individual. They now are taking a notice-me attitude." A town official asks, "How can we get and keep them back into the mainstream of our orderly social and civic life?" Not easily, as it turned out—over the next few years the newspaper is filled with accounts of the police busting up "pot parties," with "blaring rock'n'roll, marijuana cigarettes, and plenty of whiskey and beer." (One week the crime blotter reported two local youths who had "cooked marijuana in the oven at one of their homes.") By 1968, "a long-haired Lexington High School male student was sent home and told not to come back without his locks properly shorn. After he complied and returned to school, students circulated protest petitions noting the hair length of Mozart and Paul Revere."

The town struggled gamely to keep up with a changing world: by 1970, the year I arrived, the first dead soldier had come back from Vietnam in a coffin, and Ralph Nader appeared in town to give the library's annual lecture, blasting both air pollution and hot dogs, which he called "innovations to relieve food companies of all their crud." A ban on that suddenly-not-so-miraculous DDT went into effect on January 1 of the new decade, and barrels were placed outside the Department of Public Works barn to collect the pesticide. The selectmen—one of whom was now a woman—declared January 15 Martin Luther King Day.

So consider all that as the backdrop to the two events I want to describe. This is a town that has grown quickly in population and prosperity, a town that prizes education and modernity, a town struggling to come to terms with rapid change, in a country where new kinds of people are making new kinds of demands that thrill some and worry, even anger, others. It's a place that's going to have to make some choices.

THING ONE HAPPENED in Lexington over Memorial Day weekend of 1971, and it's one of the first "public" memories stored in my brain. Most of the things I can recall over the previous nine years of my life are private, events that involved me and my family, not history. This involved both—indeed, it involved my father and the largest mass arrest in state history.

The war in Vietnam had increasingly divided Lexington—thousands had turned out as early as 1966 to rally on the Common for a moratorium in the fighting. "Peace at any cost is not the American dream," the newspaper had editorialized in response, and indeed a year later two high school students organized a demonstration in support of the troops that drew three thousand to the same spot. But all this was prelude: in May of 1971, the Vietnam Veterans Against the War, led by a young and lanky John Kerry, announced plans to follow Paul Revere's route in reverse. The group obtained the okay to camp on Friday night near the bridge in Concord, and then they asked Lexington's selectmen for permission to bivouac on the Battle Green the next night. "Lexington could be a South Vietnamese or Laotian village," they said; like the minutemen of 1775, South Vietnamese guerillas were "simply fighting for the privilege to determine their own destiny," and to "exist apart from foreign domination."

But Lexington Green had a ten p.m. curfew, and the Board of Selectmen refused to lift it. The veterans would be allowed to march single file through the town, and they could hand out leaflets as long as they did not litter the sidewalks, but the chair of the board, a lifelong resident and nursing-home administrator named Robert Cataldo, said, "The Board agreed that no good purpose could be served by the demonstration or the encampment." From their Friday encampment in Concord the veterans voted to defy the order, and to bivouac on the Green the next night.

My parents were not firebrands—my mother was not part of the 29.1 percent of Lexington women who were now working outside the home, and my father was a business journalist. But they were good liberals, and firm believers in civics education, and so we went down to the Green as a family late that Saturday afternoon. The veterans had not yet arrived, and the streets were largely clear—but I can remember the menacing sound and sight of a contingent of men on motorcycles circling the Green, Hells Angels patches easy to read on their backs. Word came that a meeting would soon be underway at Town Hall, and so we walked the four blocks through the center of town. Past Cary Library, where I was already a regular in the downstairs children's room; past Brigham's, the town's ice cream parlor. Past Michelson Shoes, and the Pewter Pot coffee shop, with thirty different muffins on the menu. Past the barber shop, where there were known to be copies of *Playboy* in the stack of *Sports Illustrated*s and *Field and Stream*s, past the Bargain Barn where you went for back-to-school shopping; past the Chinese restaurant and the Italian restaurant because that was ethnic food in 1970; past the commuter train station and the Lexington Savings Bank, where I already had a passbook; past the movie theater where *Love Story* was dominating the box office that spring—all the while joining a growing stream of people headed the same direction.

Town Hall, where we were bound, needs to be a big building, because like many New England villages, Lexington governs itself via "Town Meeting." It's not the pure kind you find in little Vermont hamlets, where everyone shows up one Tuesday in March to argue and vote; at thirty thousand residents, Lexington had outgrown that kind of direct democracy. But its citizens still elected a veritable parliament—203 legislators from nine precincts—and this white building was where they sat each spring. That Saturday night, however, anyone could come in, and so we did—the selectmen were holding an informational meeting to explain why they'd blocked the veterans from camping on the Green. Perhaps because I'd never seen anything remotely like it before, the air seemed to crackle—adults were emotional, out of control in ways entirely unfamiliar to me. I remember Selectman Cataldo saying something, and before he could finish, a woman rising out of her chair to scream—*scream*—"You speak with forked tongue!" Again: this was happening a long time ago, in a different galaxy. The ad in the paper that week for the local dry cleaner had a drawing of a well-dressed man under the legend:

"My Position Demands a Neat Appearance. It's a Clever Wife Who Sees to It That All My Suits, Slacks, Jackets, and Coats Are Taken Regularly to the Professional Cleansers at Craft."

We walked the four blocks back to the Green, and by now it was dark, with the flash of red and blue lights from the tops of police cars providing the only illumination. Knots of men, many of them in faded army fatigues and almost all with beards or drooping moustaches, bunched among the trees—the orange flicker of burning cigarette ends marked the small huddles, and a sweet smell, again entirely unfamiliar, hung in the air. Local residents stood in their own knots—it was dark, but my parents greeted neighbors, parents of my fifth-grade classmates, friends from church. I did not want to leave—this was the most exciting and dangerous place I'd ever been—but I was ten, and my brother was eight, and pretty soon we were in the Plymouth, my mother at the wheel, heading home to Middle Street.

Without my father, who stayed behind on the Green. The selectmen held a last-ditch meeting with the town's clergy, almost all of whom backed the protesters, but the officials wouldn't budge, and so at three a.m. the police peacefully rounded up 458 protesters, most of them the marching veterans but including about 170 townspeople, including Gordon McKibben. They took them by bus to the town's Department of Public Works shed, where they waited amid the snowplows and garbage trucks to be processed for disorderly conduct. It remains the largest single act of civil disobedience in Bay State history, stretching back to the colonial era and up through Black Lives Matter.

My parents played it down—they weren't particularly dramatic souls, and I imagine they didn't want to alarm me and my brother. In my recollection, my father was home for breakfast by the time I woke up that Sunday morning, and I have no doubt we were soon off to church. In retrospect, I'm even more impressed now by his courage than I was then—he worked for *Business Week* magazine, after all, in an era when reporters were not encouraged to have political opinions, much less follow them to jail.

But that old order was shifting, or so it seemed. "Up until that point, Lexington had the reputation for being somewhat of a conservative community," Joseph O'Leary—at the time of the arrests a nineteen-year-old police cadet, and later a lieutenant on the force—told an oral history project years later. "After that the political environment changed, and Lexington got the reputation of being much more liberal," he said. "I think the complexion of the entire town and the people in town changed." So it seemed. Despite a stern editorial in the paper ("where on Saturday night many of the townspeople lost their dignity to the side of protest, the Selectmen gained in stature. They had the courage to uphold the law"), its letters column bulged with anger directed at town officials: fifty-five letters the week after the arrest, forty-five letters the week after that, an outpouring entirely without precedent. "I want to express my sense of outrage at the incompetent, blundering, insensitive handling by the Selectmen." "Was Paul Revere charged with disturbing the peace?" Digging through the blizzard of letters, I was pleased to see one from my address: "Lexington has always traded heavily on its symbolism as the birthplace of American liberty," my parents wrote. "Officials may as well get used to the idea that all Americans, not just a few taxpayers living here, take the slogan seriously."

Here's how the newspaper editor, Anne Scigliano, recollected it when she was interviewed for the oral history project twenty years later: "I feel that it divided the town. People became labeled as conservatives or liberals based on their actions or their sides in this particular event."

And here's the chair of the selectmen, Robert Cataldo, who had been born in Lexington in 1924 and grew up on one of those farms that were now subdivisions, describing that Saturday night meeting that stuck so firmly in my mind: "The thing got completely out of hand. I never saw so many people congregate in the town of Lexington so fast. We could spend a hundred million dollars at Town Meeting and there wouldn't have been half the people that showed up. . . . You know, not all of the people, but a great number of people that really don't know me. They just formed their opinion based on that one decision, and they're still holding it."

Reading through those oral histories, I came across a particularly thoughtful one from a woman named Bonnie Jones, who lived four houses down Middle Street from me. I'd later babysit for her children, and take care of their family iguana when they went away on vacation. "We went through that whole time of our lives in the fifties which was so unbelievably deadly boring, so there was a big appeal to have all this stuff happening. These younger people were doing all these wild things, and it was pretty seductive stuff for us. The mature part of me— and I think I had some maturity at the time—was there out of conviction and strong opposition to the war. Another part of me—that missed my adolescence—enjoyed the hell out of being there because it was exciting, and the energy was a very seductive thing."

Ten-year-old me certainly felt that way: everything seemed to be changing, and fast. I became an antiwar activist, hampered only slightly by the fact that I knew nothing about the war. (I could never remember who were our allies, the South Vietnamese or the North; then again, it was this same year that I was shocked to find out there were not two huge cities on the West Coast, one called Los Angeles and the other Ellay.) But it seemed to me that getting arrested clearly worked: by the time I was starting junior high we were pulling out of Saigon.

And so the future was clear: peace was coming. We were on the edge there in Lexington. Nothing would be the same; the old order, with its dry cleaning, was passing, and the future spread forth in all its glory. If you wanted to keep up with the Joneses, four doors down, you needed an iguana. What could stop us?

THING TWO PLAYED out over the same spring, but I knew nothing about it till I started reading archived issues of the newspaper and those detailed oral histories, to refresh my memory of that Battle Green protest. This second thing was, on its face, less dramatic, but I came to have a strong—and sinking—feeling it might have been more consequential.

In the oral histories of that night of protest, Bonnie Jones from down our street talks about moving to Lexington back in 1963,

> because it was a sort of countryish town, and offered a lot of the amenities we were looking for—a good school system, some space, and so forth, and looked like a nice town to live in.

We met people fairly quickly after we moved in. I joined the
Civil Rights Committee, the Fair Housing Committee. . . . I
remember the first meeting I went to—I signed up to track
cheap houses in town that could be available for black families that might want to move to the suburbs. I went through
the listing and found all the houses for less than $20,000 and
listed them. Then we would talk to people who were interested
in having help finding housing.

Hmm.

A few pages later in those archives, the interviewers sit down
with Nancy Earsy, who had been president of the League of
Women Voters at the time of the protests. The League was something I knew about—my mom had edited its newsletter for a few
years, and I can recall stapling and addressing six hundred copies
on the dining room table each time it came out. In any event,
Earsy describes the peace-sign earrings she wore to the Battle
Green that night, and the smell of lilacs in the air, and the grease
on the floor of the DPW barn where the arrestees were taken.
Almost as an afterthought, she was asked if there were other
"divisive" issues in town. "Low- and moderate-income housing,"
she said. "The big argument at the time was that a lot of people
were not in favor; they felt there shouldn't be apartment houses in
Lexington; it should be single-family houses." Hmm again.

Since a suburb is basically a collection of houses, it stands
to reason that who would get to live in those houses and what
kind of houses they would be would be fundamental suburban
issues—maybe the most fundamental issues, even more so than

the distant war. And so it was in Lexington, as a closer reading began to make clear.

Lexington was, it probably goes without saying, overwhelmingly white. "Restrictive covenants" had limited housing access in such communities for centuries—historians point out that as early as the 1790s a minister in nearby Salem, Massachusetts, had complained that the presence of a "negro hut" was damaging the neighborhood. Such deed restrictions were common in the suburbs by the 1920s; after the war, federal housing loans under the GI bill and "redlining" by banks to restrict loans kept many areas off-limits. By the early 1960s, with the civil rights movement spreading, some people were starting to feel bad about such practices—in 1962, fourteen hundred Lexingtonians signed a "good neighbor" pledge stating, "I will accept families and individuals into my neighborhood without discrimination because of religion, color, or national origin." As the newspaper boasted, "Lexington, the birthplace of American liberty, is still its ardent champion." Noting that a wide range of townspeople had signed on—"from banker to brickmason, fireman to fundraiser, meat smoker to meteorologist, physician to postman, sculptor to steamfitter, and treasurer to truck driver,"—it concluded, "Lexington citizens, like their forebears, still believe in 'liberty and justice for all,' and are ready to support the practice, as well as the principles, of fair housing."

But of course the right to a house is not quite the same thing *as* a house, and as the decade wore on and the price of homes in Lexington rose, it became pretty clear that the town wasn't, in fact, becoming more diverse. After the assassination of Martin Luther

King in 1968, some of the town's leading lights formed the marvelously named Suburban Responsibility Commission and began figuring out ways to change. Working with the local Council of Churches, the commission shaped plans fairly quickly. The fundamental reality was that "single-family homes" of the type that filled Lexington, each with its own driveway and yard, were essentially incompatible with "low- and moderate-income housing"; if you wanted cheaper homes, you needed to group them together, in clusters small and large. By 1969 there were plans for a first batch of 115 "garden apartments" to be sold to people of moderate income at a site off one of the town's main roads, adjacent to the railroad tracks and to a cemetery. The town Planning Board, at an informational hearing, pointed out that Lexington comprised about 1.1 percent of the metro Boston area, and hence "our minimum proportional share of new low and moderate-income dwellings" should be about 330 units: this one development would take care of about 35 percent of the town's "suburban responsibility."

The town fathers were lined up firmly behind the plans, even if there were a few ominous signs. (At an early Planning Board meeting, a few neighbors of the proposed complex stood to register their complaints. One said he'd be fine with the plan "if it wasn't right on top of me"; another said, "Everyone does not have to live in Lexington—Lexington is not Mecca." He was suspicious of the whole plan, he added, because "this is the way slums start.") Still, momentum seemed strong. First the Planning Board approved the proposal, and then, in early April of 1971, Town Meeting—that local parliament that meets for a few Monday nights each spring—gave its blessing, 127–56, passing the necessary two-thirds bar.

And then something happened that didn't happen very often in Lexington. Unsatisfied with the deliberation of Town Meeting, neighbors of the proposed project signed petitions in sufficient numbers to force a town-wide referendum on the project—a ballot to be held within a few weeks. "This step has not been used often," the editor of the newspaper opined, "but it is available in cases where there may be a sharp difference between the town meeting members and the public at large. It is a part of our governing process, and is a final assurance of the complete democratic procedure." That democratic process was reflected in the letters pages of the newspaper over the next two weeks. "Although this approach to housing is admittedly somewhat new for Lexington, it is a 1971 solution to a 1971 problem," one resident wrote, and "a significant step forward in human relations." The parish council at Saint Brigid's, the local Catholic church, weighed in in favor; so did Roland Greeley, a local icon who had served on the Planning Board beginning in the 1930s. There were a few complaints from people who said it would place too much pressure on schools, but they were far outweighed by residents insisting that the time had come for Lexington to change. Mr. Myron Miller of 46 Eldred Street, for instance:

If the referendum overturns the seriously considered vote of your Town Meeting members, it will really be because of certain unfounded fears of "those welfare people" and "hoodlums from the city." First of all, the only element you might get from the city is that from which most of us come—the element that wants to improve its life by coming to the suburbs.

And if we're really honest with ourselves, we in Lexington hold no great monopoly on uprightness than anybody else. We have bullies, drug users (and pushers, too, most likely), marital squabbles, and families doing a bad job of bringing up kids. Why don't we show that we're real Americans and take this tiny step to show that our hearts are in the right place and we have a desire to see all improve their lives?

Lexington's vote, then, was historic. It was also a landslide. "In spite of the day-long drizzle, 52 percent of Lexington's 15,317 registered voters went to the polls and voted nearly two to one against approving the action of their representative Town Meeting to rezone land for the proposed Centre Village. A total of 7,981 votes were cast: 2,718 were in favor of the rezoning, and 5,175 were opposed." That is to say: in public the members of Town Meeting had come out in favor of a small low-income housing complex. In public, the letters column of the local paper had broken sharply in its favor. But in the privacy of the voting booth, the townspeople had rejected it decisively. As the newspaper pointed out, turnout for the special referendum was higher than any similar vote in the past; barely a third of residents had turned out to vote in the last town election. More than a rejection of a particular project, the paper explained, the vote needed to be read as "a strong voice against subsidized housing for Lexington." If there was actually some reason to plan for "needy families" in the future, an editorial opined, "let it be done slowly and cautiously."

· · · · ·

LIFE RETURNED TO suburban normal after these two massive fights—within weeks the selectmen were at work on a new sewer plan, the League of Women Voters had collected 1,037 pounds of tin cans for a new project called "recycling," and the largest class in the history of Lexington High School graduated after listening to senior class vice president Sylvia Notini of 2 Blueberry Lane ask, "Why it is that so much anger, hatred, and grief can be caused by the color of a person's skin, why a thing called war must exist, and why one man throws out a piece of half-eaten steak while another rolls on the ground slowly dying of starvation?"

Good questions, those. Mine now are not so different. What was the actual place where I grew up? Was it the place where 170 townspeople joined those restive veterans to be arrested on the Green? Or was it the place where 5,175 people turned out to make sure that no homes for poor people would be built in their town?

I've spent much of my life believing that Thing One—that scene on the Common, lit by the whirling lights of police cars and the earnest hopes of a liberal populace—represented the real image of my generation, symbol of a moment of liberation and transformation that reshaped American politics and culture. If that spark was dimmed over the years—if the country took a turn toward Reaganism, toward endless consumption, toward the ugliness that was Trump—those seemed to me like detours, deviations from the main path. In my mind, my generation was, and would remain, the generation that came of age amid hope and change (and I've lived my life as if that were true, working to build new movements, following my father to jail over and over).

It's not an impossible argument: right now some of that old hope is reasserting itself. Joe Biden, a man who joined the Senate the year after these events took place, is now pushing America to live up to that image, though his efforts are running into the country's polarized division, not to mention the filibuster. It feels a little as if history, having hiccupped, has resumed.

But even if our country somehow manages to steady itself now, an astonishing amount of damage has been done in the intervening half century—scads of lives blighted by inequality, our democracy endangered, and the planet itself badly scarred, perhaps beyond salvation. And, disproportionately, that damage has been done by the generation that grew up in those suburbs in those years. Extraordinary wealth accumulated in those places and in that generation, but it wasn't used to build a better country. The sense of national unity dwindled; the religious faith that had helped order communities melted away. Mass prosperity itself turned into the most dangerous weapon of all, unleashing the flood of carbon that raised the temperature of the earth till the poles thawed. Looking back, Thing Two—that referendum vote—perfectly symbolizes the hyper-individualism that has marked my lifetime. The selfishness.

Perhaps something of that old world—of the flag, the cross, and the station wagon—can be summoned up again to help us face a difficult future by repairing the damage they helped cause. Perhaps the generation that began its life in those suburbs, and is now moving slowly to retirement communities, can recapture what was so promising about those beginnings. But if so, we'll need to deal honestly with some serious questions. That's what this book is about.

THE FLAG

· · · · · · ·

Do you know how to make the colonial-era cocktail called "flip"? Combine rum, porter, egg, cream, and molasses, and then plunge a heated iron bar—a loggerhead—into the mug to heat it. (Do you know where the expression "at loggerheads" comes from? You do now.)

I can remember that recipe and that small joke because I repeated it, in a loud voice, three or four or five times a day for several summers—it was a set-piece in the half-hour spiel that I delivered to tourists who descended on the Battle Green each day. I was one among the small corps of officially licensed guides, all Lexington high school kids, who wore tricorne hats and sat on a bench behind the statue of the Minuteman, playing the board game Risk and waiting for the next crowd to arrive. When it was your turn, you led them off around the Common— maybe one family with a couple of bored teenagers, maybe an entire bus of Japanese tourists. You told them the story of that day in April when the local farmers took on the British army in the first engagement of the American Revolution, and then, when you were done, you held out your tricorne hat and collected your pay in the form of tips.

To qualify as a guide you needed to pass a test, which was administered by the venerable rector of the local Episcopal church, a man who had been in that pulpit since the 1930s. He handed you a reading list, and you repaired to the town library's local history room for long days of study. Some of that reading list was about the battle itself—who got shot and how—and some of it was about the history of the town, and some of it was about the meaning of the Revolution. We took it seriously. The head guide, a year ahead of me in school, was a boy named Richard John, who went on to become one of the leading American historians of the era, now on the faculty at Columbia. He was a ham as well as a historian—his tours were legendary, and in the course of a summer he cleared the equivalent of $10,000 today. (He also, however, had to deal with the fallout from the rest of his staff—one tourist, for instance, memorably complained to the Chamber of Commerce that his guide was a communist, because he'd implied that the minutemen had been drinking the night of the battle.) The rest of us made far less, but it was still a good summer job, out in the open air, learning to speak in public.

And learning, too, to think of American history in a certain way. I've been a patriot ever since, though of a particular kind. If the American origin story that you're telling over and over involves a small force of ill-trained men who, feeling oppressed, decide to take on the greatest empire in the world—well, that story leaves you believing that dissent can be patriotic, that American history is ultimately the story of the underdog, that a sense of shared community and a willingness to sacrifice for it defines who we are. Because of that I've always been both amazed and chagrined that many progressives willingly surrendered the flag to the Right— that in their dislike for much of what we'd become they overlooked how we'd begun, and in the process gave the other side its most valuable prop. Why should the stars and stripes belong to men who believed in individualism over community, who were building new empires as oppressive as anything the British had constructed? Didn't it make more sense, as the Vietnam Veterans Against the War had recognized, to claim that symbol as sacred, and to insist that it undercut the powers that be? I was a guide on the Green during the Bicentennial year, when visitors streamed in like never before, so I told the same old story again and again until it was deeply imprinted on me. And I never lost that sense of connection to an apparently noble past. In my mind, I think, the movements that I've helped build over the years were like nonviolent versions of that scene on the Green.

What I'm trying to say is that I came by my patriotism honestly. Which is why it's been hard, over the last decade or two, to absorb the new iterations of history that view our past in far deeper shadow, to embrace the history that informed and led up to, say, the 1619 Project, and its insistence that American history is best seen as an (ongoing) story of repression. Those new histories are persuasive—they explain a great deal about who we are right now as a nation—and they've deeply complicated my old understanding. And I think I'm not alone. Those new interpretations have provoked a backlash from right-wingers insistent on clinging to old stories, and a sense of shame from the rest of us—shame at our past, shame that we hadn't reckoned with it.

The debate over the flag—over whether it's possible to be a patriotic American, to look at our history with some pride and draw on it as an inspiration for our future—is above all a question about race in America. That's what this section of the book is about.

But it will take a while to get there because I'm going to start this chapter of the book by explaining how the story of the

American Revolution sat in my mind for most of my life—not just the battle of Lexington, but its context and meaning. Then I'm going to hold that up against the emerging understandings of our history, the new set of facts about race and class, about enslaved people and Native people (the people who weren't in my old spiel, at least as main characters). And then I'm going to try to see what there is to salvage from that past: what reparations we must make before we can try to tell that story once more in ways that might help us be a little revolutionary again.

I'm not going to hurry through this. When we guided on the Green, we had to go fast: the great fear was that halfway through your spiel the bus driver would blow his horn and your crowd would clamber back aboard the Greyhound for the trip down the road to Concord before you had a chance to pass the hat and collect your pay. But since you can put this book down when you need to, and then return to it later, I feel no need to compress the story too much. If it helps to imagine me wearing a tricorne hat as I lecture at you, please feel free.

LEXINGTON, WE WOULD tell visitors, had originally been called Cambridge Farms, a rural precinct of the Puritan settlement along the Charles River. By the mid-1630s, colonists were trampling through the area—the main street through the region, Massachusetts Avenue, began life as the path out from Boston for the congregation that settled Concord. Over the next 150 years, Lexington and its surrounding towns were slowly settled. As the historian George Daughan put it, "Economic opportunity was widespread, and upward mobility common. There was an abundance of land. Anyone willing to work hard could accumulate the money to buy enough acreage for a farm, which was the key to a prosperous life." (I don't think we guides ever made mention of who had used this land before; I honestly can't remember if that's because it seemed shamefully obvious, or because, far more shamefully, it never occurred to us. But I suspect the latter). Ninety percent of the population farmed, and by some accounts, "no agricultural society in the world was as prosperous as that of the country people in the Bay Colony." The seaports of Massachusetts—Boston, but also New Bedford, Marblehead, and the rest—hummed, exporting the produce of those farms and even ice carved from the region's ponds and packed in sawdust.

Democracy in these settlements was broad—not, perhaps, compared to now, but compared to the world in the eighteenth century. Town Meeting decided most of the important questions: where and when to build bridges and schools and roads, but also which minister to hire for the local meetinghouse that was the center of public life. "Would the sheep be allowed on the common? Could hogs still run at large? A large part of local government was devoted to keeping one man's livestock out of another man's fields." Indeed in many communities the "fence-viewer" was a crucial elected official. To vote in Massachusetts town elections, says the historian Robert Gross, one needed to be a male of twenty-one years, a resident for the last year, and the owner of property that would rent for three pounds a year, which was not a huge sum—the equivalent of about a month's wages. In Concord, for instance, in the years before the Revolution, seven out of ten men qualified. "Those who could not were farmers' sons only recently come of age, and day laborers and servants, dependent on others for their bread." (And of course people who'd been enslaved, but more on that to come.) The theory was that no one should vote who wasn't his own man—thus preventing large landowners with lots of servants from dominating public life.

Nonetheless, towns usually opted to make affluent local landowners their selectmen and their representatives to the General Court in Boston; among other things, these were the men who could afford to take the time off for such duties. And such men tended toward a kind of native conservatism—they were not inclined to rock the boat. In a sense, however, their mere existence was a threat to the authorities back in England, where only one man in six could vote, and only one in five owned land; to London the prosperity and relative independence of places like Massachusetts was grating. A typical American paid no more than sixpence a year to the Crown in taxes, according to the historian Rick Atkinson—about a fiftieth of the average tax burden of an Englishman, even though the Royal Navy kept the oceans safe for American trade, and British regiments guarded the frontiers against Indian encroachment. Still, colonists regarded even these modest levies as a hateful imposition. When, in 1765, the British passed the Stamp Act, a tax on everything written on paper from playing cards to wills, the reaction was fierce: revenue officers were attacked, and boycotts on imports closed British factories. The law was repealed a year later, and the colonies burst out in revels "from Boston to Savannah, with fireworks and much bad celebratory verse." The British kept trying, however—with taxes on lead, on glass, on paint. When Bostonians protested the measures, London sent regiments, who in 1770 killed five in the Boston Massacre. After the inevitable backlash the British acquiesced again, repealing every tax save the one on tea, which they left in place mainly to assert Parliament's authority.

That authority was hard to maintain across an ocean. In December 1773, Lexingtonians—at the urging of their long-time minister Jonas Clarke (for whom the town would, in 1970, name its new junior high school, which I was in the first class to attend)—searched their homes for tea, burning it in a large bonfire. Three days later Bostonians, "dressed in the Indian manner," their faces blacked, carried out the more famous tea party, boarding three merchant ships and pouring forty-five tons of tea into the Harbor, by torchlight and amid war whoops. Local silversmith Paul Revere mounted his horse and carried news of the event to New York and Philadelphia. Soon word reached London, where King George said, "I am much hurt." Hurt enough that in the spring of 1774 Parliament adopted four laws known to the British as the Coercive Acts and to America as the Intolerable Acts. These measures closed the port of Boston till restitution had been paid for the tea, and also essentially ended democracy in Massachusetts: Town Meetings would be restricted, the elected governing council for the colony would henceforth be appointed by the governor, and royal officials accused of serious crimes would now be tried back in England. With the old colonial charter abrogated, a military man— General Thomas Gage—was named to head what Atkinson called "the arbitrary new regime."

Predictably, this went over badly. On June 5, 1774, Dr. Joseph Warren, Sam Adams's protégé in Boston's Sons of Liberty, sent out a letter to all the colonies to join a Solemn League and Covenant to boycott all British goods. In a world that traveled at horse speed, the first replies came from the nearest towns— within days, eight of them, including Lexington, had pledged their support. By autumn Lexington was preparing for its defense, buying two half barrels of gunpowder (which was stored in the church) and beginning to drill its militia (all able-bodied men aged sixteen to fifty) on the Common. King George, too, was preparing for a fight. "When once these rebels have felt a smart blow, they will submit," he predicted confidently.

In the event, he was wrong. These minutemen were not trained soldiers like the redcoats (though they had a certain kind of discipline—any Lexington militiaman who interrupted the clerk while he was calling the roll was fined two shillings). But they were part of a close-knit society that had a strong sense of its destiny. It was a *small* society, with the same few families dominating. In Lexington, the patriot Reverend Clarke had succeeded the patriot Rev. John Hancock, grandfather of the famous Hancock. (Indeed, it was in the town parsonage his widowed grandmother still inhabited that the younger Hancock was staying with Sam Adams on the night before the battle; warning them was Paul Revere's first task.) Down the road in Concord, meanwhile, Rev. William Emerson—grandfather to Ralph Waldo—was in the pulpit, and he preached over the first muster of the town's minutemen. Soldiers, he said, should not enlist in "order to make a pompous appearance" or to "look big and to stalk proudly." Instead the soldier's purpose was "the Honour of God and the good of his Country."

And so it came to pass. In Boston, General Gage was feeling

hemmed in, and London was pressing him to act. In April he decided to send troops on a night raid to seize arms he believed the colonials were storing in Concord. A pre-raid scouting expedition was inept; forewarned, the locals hid the weapons and began preparing for the fight. Revere, famously, worked out his signals, and on the night of April 18, as a compatriot hung two lanterns in the steeple of Boston's Old North Church to signify that the Brits were proceeding by water, he paddled with muffled oars across the Charles, found a waiting mount, and proceeded on his famous ride to warn the countryside. It's likely that instead of "the British are coming," he was shouting, "The regulars are coming out," but in any event it worked. It took him two hours to cover the eleven miles to Lexington—he had to veer around British sentinels—and as he galloped in to warn Hancock and Adams to flee, he also spread the word to the town militia. Soon the bell on Belfry Hill next to the Green was ringing, and men were assembling in the chill night. Chill enough that, as there was no immediate sign of approaching troops, they repaired fifty yards to Buckman Tavern and its store of flip.

Eventually, toward dawn, word came that the British troops were finally nearing, and eighty minutemen filtered out of the tavern and took up a kind of a ragged line across the two-acre Common, behind the church that stood at its head. They were obviously outnumbered and outgunned, up against the most feared army on the earth—and they weren't idiots. They didn't block the road to Concord, where the British were going; they stood aside to watch. John Parker, commander of this small force, was forty-five years old; he'd fought under the British in the French and Indian War before coming home to farm. (And he had tuberculosis, which would kill him before the year was out.) He was in charge of men he'd known his whole life, and so—despite legend—he almost certainly did not say, "If they mean to have a war, then let it begin here." He was trying to avoid trouble.

As best as anyone can tell, the commander of the British advance guard, a marine officer named John Pitcairn, also told his men not to fire; to the minutemen he yelled, "Throw down your arms, ye villains, ye rebels," and "Disperse, ye rebels." Parker testified later that he'd ordered his militia to do just that, and likely some did begin to drift away. And then a single shot, fired by no one knows who, sounded out. That touched it off; almost immediately, in Rick Atkinson's account, "muskets quickly barked along the British line, promiscuous shooting from agitated soldiers."

Before British officers managed to bring their troops under control, eight minutemen had been killed and nine wounded. We told those stories day after day on the Green: Jonas Parker, cousin to the captain and at fifty-three one of the oldest men on the Green, got off a shot, dropped his tricorne hat to the ground, and filled it with his flints, preparing to fire again. Before he could, a British regular ran him through with a bayonet. Or consider Jonathan Harrington, aged thirty. (He was one of eight Harringtons on the Green—this was, again, a tight-knit community; a quarter of the minutemen on the Green were related by blood or marriage to Captain Parker.) Shot close to his house on the western edge of the Common, he managed—or so the myth had it—to drag himself the distance to his doorstep, where he died at his wife's feet.

Eventually the British officers found a drummer, and the

sound of him beating the call to order brought the redcoats to their senses. With huzzahs they re-formed their ranks and stepped off on the six-mile march to Concord. They left behind a gory scene—"Lexington had not been a battle, or even a skirmish, but an execution," in Atkinson's words, and only two British privates (and Pitcairn's horse) had even been nicked by colonial bullets. But never mind; it was the start. Sam Adams, who had made good his escape with Hancock and their papers, was still close enough to town to hear the gunfire. "Oh, what a glorious morning for America," he supposedly said, which became Lexington's official motto.

That "glorious" morning turned into a long, long day—at least as long for the British as for the minutemen. As the alarm spread, militias from surrounding towns began to gather and then to march. Some of them reached Concord in time to join the fight at North Bridge, which saw the first redcoats die. Many more took up positions along the road that they knew the British would have to use for their return to Boston, the road that ran back through Lexington. Parker had lost many men that morning, but the Lexingtonians who remained alive were angry. They lurked in the trees on a ridge about two miles west of the Green, pouring fire on the British and then evaporating into the forest to set up the next ambush and the next. By the time the regulars made it back into the center of Lexington they were on the edge of annihilation, exhausted and low on ammunition. Only then did reinforcements appear from Boston—a thousand fresh troops, with heavy cannon. The artillery scattered the minutemen (and put a hole in the meetinghouse); the troops were able to regroup and even to do some looting, carrying off what they

could from surrounding houses. Even with the cover of the big
guns, though, the retreat back to their barracks in the safety of
Boston was a narrow thing—they were fired on the whole way,
with scores of dead on both sides.

The world changed that day. The British, whose empire was
the greatest on earth, had been routed by a tangle of farmers who
improvised their tactics and shifted leadership on the fly. "Who-
ever looks upon them as an irregular mob, will find himself very
much mistaken," Lieutenant-General Hugh Percy, who had organized the relief column with the cannon, wrote to his superiors
in London. "They have men amongst them who knew very well
what they are about." The colonials, meanwhile, knew exactly how
to make use of the day's events: Paul Revere and a host of other
riders fanned out up and down the seaboard, making sure everyone knew that "Gage has fired upon the people." It took a few
weeks for the news to make it south to Georgia and the Carolinas,
but the stories grew more lurid as they traveled: families burned
alive, pregnant women bayoneted. "Stunning success at the battle
of Lexington and Concord brought the colonies together as never
before," George Daughan wrote in his account of the battle.
"Doubts about whether they stood a chance against the British
colossus lessened dramatically." Soon George Washington was en
route to Boston to take command of the troops, and the great
war was underway—a war that stretched on for eight long years,
through Bunker Hill and Brooklyn, through Saratoga and Valley
Forge, through Savannah and Charlestown and finally Yorktown.

That was the account we guides would deliver as we strolled
the Green in our tricorne hats (and as we knelt to reenact the
bayoneting of poor Jonas Parker). It was a clean and brave story,

and, as I say, it has informed me ever since. The valor of standing up to unjust and arbitrary power seemed to me its clear and obvious moral. Indeed, in the years that followed, as I read more deeply in American history, the importance of that stand sank further in.

I want to talk about that—to tell how and why the Revolution came to seem so important to me. I want to draw the picture in as bold lines as possible. Because soon enough the picture is going to get much more shaded, much less noble. But not quite yet.

OUR FAMILY CAME to Lexington from a five-year sojourn in Canada—in Toronto, where my father covered the country for *Business Week*, and where I started school. There was much to like about Canada—as time has gone by I've grown more grateful for having those formative years in a country that took community seriously. (National health care, imagine that!) But Canada in the 1960s was still a pretty provincial place, where the Crown was taken seriously. My first day at school, having arrived straight from my native California, I was sent—bewildered—to the principal's office, to be strapped. (Lightly, but still.) My offense: I hadn't doffed my cap when entering the (boys'!) entrance to the school, which showed "disrespect to the Queen." I've never felt more rebelliously American in my life.

So let me tell you about the book I read many years later that helped cement my vision of the Revolution, helped drive deep the lessons about the rustic nobility of that stand by the minutemen. Gordon Wood is among the most important of American historians. Born one town over in Concord, he won the Pulitzer for his 1991 volume *The Radicalism of the American Revolution*, which is I think the greatest of his books. It describes the psychological meaning of the Revolution for those who participated, and for the society they built. "Mid-eighteenth century colonial society was in many ways still traditional," he wrote. "Traditional in its basic social relationships and in its cultural consciousness. . . . Authority and liberty flowed not as today from the political organization of the society but from the structure of its personal relationships." And those relationships were highly structured indeed. "Living in a monarchical society meant, first of all, being subjects of the king. This was no simple political status, but had all sorts of social, cultural, and even psychological implications." The king was a father, and so on down through the ranks. As the contemporary poet Alexander Pope put it:

> Order is Heaven's first law; and this confest,
> Some are, and must be, greater than the rest.

The governors of the colonies, who were as close as most Americans would ever come to the throne, put on airs to impress their power on their subjects: "by building distinguished government houses, by dressing lavishly, by entertaining generously." But those were not the only hierarchies. College students, for instance, were taught to remove their hats at varying distances from the person they approached, depending on the status of that person: fifty yards from the president, forty yards from a professor, twenty-five from a tutor. The difference between the aristocracy and the ordinary was so great that "many still thought the two orders represented two orders of being." Gentlemen and commoners had "different psyches, different emotional makeups, different natures." Even George Washington referred to ordinary farmers as "the grazing multitude." Gentlemen, by contrast, wore wigs or powdered their hair, they studied the classics, and they were *free*, above all free of the need to labor like the bulk of the population. Far better to *have* a living then to make one; even Benjamin Franklin, epitome of industriousness, wrote: "Who is there that can be handsomely Supported in Affluence, Ease and Pleasure by another, that will chuse rather to earn his Bread by the Sweat of His own Brows?" (Franklin, in fact, retired from the printing trade at forty-two and set himself up as a man of leisure, content to engage in science and diplomacy rather than commerce.) Reputation was valued above all—hence the epidemic of dueling, almost always to preserve a good name.

The British troops were the dregs of their society, but they were officered by gentlemen, and this was thought to make all the difference. As Lord Percy, clear-eyed brigade commander in Boston, put it, "I never believed, I confess, that they would have attacked the King's troops."

And yet they did. A kind of rough equality had been building on those New England farms, amid the general prosperity. And when it came to the fore, it did so with a bang. A year after the battle of Lexington, the most powerful men in America came together to sign a document that declared "all men are created equal." We've heard the phrase so often that it doesn't fully resonate anymore (or it echoes with hypocrisy). But against the backdrop of that hierarchical world, divided in ways we can scarcely imagine between betters and commoners, it was pure dynamite. America was born in a burst of radical egalitarianism,

determined to end the systems of preference that until just yes-
terday had seemed so natural. "Everywhere men expressed their
anger over the exclusive and unresponsive governments that had
distributed offices, land, and privileges to favorites." Passionate
emotion lay behind their constitutional declarations, like that of
the New Hampshire State Constitution's Bill of Rights, which
declared that "no office or place, whatsoever, in government,
shall be hereditary—the abilities and integrity requisite in all,
not being transmissible to posterity or relations." By the time
a generation had gone to war, with all the hardship it endured,
deference to the monarch had not just dissolved but had turned
into a hatred of kings, and of the hierarchies they represented.

Such psychological upheaval carries costs, of course—you
can find in it the roots of the anti-intellectualism that continues
to mar our society, the antagonism toward "elites" that trans-
lated into, say, Donald Trump's attacks on scientists like Dr.
Fauci or his declaration that "I love the poorly educated." But
Trump, for all his pretense of "draining the swamp," was actually
the embodiment of those old hierarchies, the exception to the
American rule. He was the man who sat (at least in his bath-
room) on a golden throne; who said, of our nation's problems, "I
alone" can solve them; who insisted that the Constitution gave
him "the right to do whatever I want." The man who installed his
family members in positions of high power, and who used occa-
sions of state to line his pockets. And if he and his compatriots
tried to use the imagery of the American Revolution to consolidate power (a "tea party" to fight against equal access to medical
care, an "insurrection" to prevent the counting of votes), then at
least for the moment the tradition of our egalitarian history still

managed to hold. It was Jamie Raskin—grandson of a Russian Jewish émigré plumber, now a congressman from Maryland—who concluded Trump's impeachment trial for that insurrection with an account of those early days of the Republic, of "our great revolutionary struggle against the kings, and queens, and the tyrants . . . Because for most of the rest of human history, it had been the kings and queens and tyrants and nobles lording it over the common people. Could political self-government work in America, was the question." He quoted from Thomas Paine: "Tyranny, like hell, is not easily conquered, but we have this saving consolation: the more difficult the struggle, the more glorious in the end will be our victory."

Raskin didn't win that legal battle, of course—the bootlickers of the Republican Party protected Trump from prosecution, and they may yet try to install him back on the throne. (How easy to imagine Lindsay Graham or Mitch McConnell in a powdered wig, packing the family silver to flee to London with the other loyalists.) But, at least for the moment, the basic outline of American history shuddered but held. That anger at arbitrary power, that refusal to allow one person to lord it over another or over the whole—that is *the* glory of American history, and it dates back, if you want a date, to those days and years immediately following the stand on the Green. It's why I've never wanted to give up the flag.

THE OBVIOUS PROBLEM with this glorification of American history is that the egalitarian impulse that drove the Revolution didn't apply to everyone. In my mind, that problem eventually had two names: Prince Estabrook and Mark Codman. They were Black men of that time and place, to whom we shall return in a moment.

To the extent that I thought about race in those middle school and high school years, it was with the happy notion that the problem was being solved. I'd understood racism as legal segregation; Martin Luther King and the movement he helped summon had struck it down; and now things were improving. It was the decade of firsts: the 1970s produced everything from the first African American in the Miss America pageant to the first African American member of the New York Stock Exchange, the first Episcopal bishop to head a diocese, the first four-star general. Surely this was what progress looked like—the first payments on that check that Dr. King, in his most famous speech, demanded be cashed against the country's original promissory note.

As the decades have worn on, however, that cheerfulness has become impossible to sustain, even for a white person who was only really looking on from a distance. In my lifetime, the country mounted what was clearly a racialized war on drugs; we built the world's largest penal system, designed largely to house Black and brown bodies; lawmakers figured out systems of gerrymandering and vote suppression to keep white political power intact; the gaps in wealth and education between Black and white America refused to close, and indeed began to widen further.

And if the present seemed grimmer than expected, *so did the past*: historians increasingly undercut the patriotic sense that egalitarianism was our birthright. Instead, they told the stories that had always been ignored, of the people who built America without recompense, of the people who never shared in her prosperity. This new historiography reached its height in 2019 when the *New York Times* devoted an entire issue of its weekly magazine to the 1619 Project, a rearguing of the nation's history led by Nikole Hannah-Jones that won the Pulitzer for its depiction of the enduring racial caste system that "aims to reframe the country's history by placing the consequences of slavery and the contributions of Black Americans at the very center of our national narrative." It was arguably the most widely read and debated piece of American history in American history, its potency proved by the reactions against it. Right-wing lawmakers scrambled to pass bills preventing schools in their states from using it in the classroom; two days before Trump finally left office, a team of conservative leaders he'd assembled to rebut the *Times* published the "1776 Report," a document so crude it might as well have been written in crayon. (It listed the chief historic threats to America's principles as slavery, but also "progressivism," which had produced "bureaucracy"; one historian told the *Washington Post* that "this 'report' lacks citations or any indication books were consulted.")

I think that the 1619 Project is a crucial document; it accomplished that rarest of feats, actually changing the way that many people understood the world. Most of it seems unarguable to me, and if I sometimes miss the less complicated American story I grew up with, I'm far more grateful for the truer picture I got in exchange. There was one sentence in the 1619 Project, however, that came under serious scrutiny by serious historians, a sentence that bears on Lexington. In her introductory essay, Hannah-Jones had written, "one of the primary reasons the colonists decided to declare their independence from Britain was because they wanted to protect the institution of slavery" against rising abolitionist sentiment in Britain; the Revolution had been fought, she contended, at least in part to "ensure that slavery would continue." If that was really true, my *entire* sense of our history, absolutely everything that I'd learned on the Green and that informed what remained of my patriotism, was an illusion, and an ugly one at that, covering up the real truth. So it was with a certain psychic relief that I watched scholars zero in on that sentence. Five eminent historians, including the same Gordon Wood I cited at length earlier, wrote to the *Times* insisting that while they "applaud all efforts to address the enduring centrality of slavery and racism," the lines about the Revolution were "not true." Leslie Harris, an African American historian, said that it was precisely because the 1619 Project was "a much-needed corrective to the blindly celebratory histories that once dominated our understanding of the past" that she had tried to warn *Times* fact-checkers that the line about the origins of the Revolution was wrong: "the protection of the slavery was not one of the main reasons the 13 Colonies went to war," and that if the paper insisted on the claim, "critics would use the overstated claim to discredit the entire undertaking." At first the *Times* refused to correct the article; as pressure from historians grew, it eventually relented a little, adding a word: protecting slavery was a reason, it now said, for *some* of the colonists to have launched the Revolution. Someone reading the original text, Hannah-Jones said, might well have assumed she meant "all 13 colonies and most people involved. And I accept that criticism, for sure."

So I suppose I might have kept my version of the American Revolution, and Lexington's honorable role in its start, partially intact in my mind. But the particular genius of Hannah-Jones and the 1619 Project is the way that it encourages you to look a little deeper, to pull on some threads, to imagine that behind the official history another version likely lurks. So: Prince Estabrook, and Mark Codman.

The first of those names I knew, if dimly. All Lexington guides had a mental list of who'd been on the Green that day, or at least who had been killed and wounded, and so I knew that Prince Estabrook, an enslaved thirty-four-year-old, was one of the nine injured in the fight. But that was it—he hadn't left much of a trail for us amateur historians to follow; we lacked dramatic stories about him with which to entertain the tourists. And possibly we didn't look too closely because slavery didn't mix very well with the story we were telling.

In the years since, scholars have tried to learn more, though the trail is murky (which tells you something about the value attached to Estabrook's life). A Lexington resident, Alice Hinkle, wrote a very short biography that covers what we know. Benjamin Estabrook, by 1775, was a distinguished citizen, serving at various times as coroner, town moderator, justice of the peace, and selectman. He also owned a slave, a single man named Prince. What exactly their relationship was like is not clear. (By one account Benjamin, a horse trader, would team up with Prince to peddle questionable stock. "One day Ben was trying to sell a rather poor horse to a back countryman, and Prince was seen walking around with tears in his eyes," begging his master not to sell the animal.) In any event, Prince Estabrook was wounded on the Green, and his wounds healed sufficiently that he was back in action two months later for the Battle of Bunker Hill in Boston; before the war was out he had signed on for expeditions to Fort Ticonderoga and to the Hudson Highlands, as well as duty guarding prisoners of war in Cambridge. His enlistment records for the various campaigns list his height from five foot six to five eleven. According to Hinkle he mustered out of the service in 1783 at West Point, and then returned to Lexington—we don't know exactly when he was freed, but a number of local Black patriots received independence in return for their service in the war. By the 1790 census he appears as a "non-white freeman" on the rolls, still living with the Estabrooks; he seems to have followed some of that family when they settled further west in Ashby, Massachusetts, where he died—maybe in 1830, maybe at the age of ninety. "No date of death or burial records, however, have been found. The records might be missing because officials did not always record such information for African Americans."

That small cache of biography is enough, however—enough to complicate my picture of the fight on Lexington Common. At least one of the men wasn't there entirely of his own accord. Prince Estabrook wasn't defending quite the same thing as Benjamin Estabrook. And if Massachusetts was not South Carolina, with vast plantations worked by barracks full of enslaved men, women, and children, slavery was not an anomaly here: there were five slaveholders in Lexington in 1775, and twenty years earlier a special census ordered by the Massachusetts General Court had found twenty-four slaves in the town. Slave owners once filled half the government posts in Concord according to local historian Elise Lemire. "This may be the birthplace of a certain kind of liberty," she said. "But Concord was a slave town. That's what it was." In the middle of the eighteenth century, a fifth of Boston families had a slave. The *Boston Gazette* may have been a patriot paper—it commissioned Paul Revere to create an engraving of the Boston Massacre and published essays from Samuel Adams under at least twenty-five different pseudonyms—but it also, the month before the battle of Lexington, ran an ad offering "a healthy Negro girl, about 20 years, remarkably good-natured and fond of children," for a price of £40.

You can get a sense of the psychological omnipresence of slavery even in New England by the number of times patriots explain why they're fighting the British: one after another, they insist that they don't want to become slaves. "Indeed," writes Gordon Wood, "they told themselves over and over that if ever they should agree to a parliamentary tax or allow their colonial assemblies to be silenced, 'nothing will remain to us but a dreadful expectation of certain slavery.'"

To their credit, enough Northerners recognized the hypocrisy of the situation that, as the Revolution wound down, these newly independent states moved to end slavery. Between 1780 and 1804, Pennsylvania, Rhode Island, Connecticut, New York, and New Jersey all passed what historian Margot Minardi called "gradual emancipation statutes." Massachusetts enacted a Declaration of Rights in 1780 stating "all men are born free and equal," but it took three years before a Supreme Court ruling confirmed that slavery no longer existed in the Commonwealth; even then, says Minardi, it may have lingered on. What definitely continued was a none-too-subtle racism. By the 1820s, politicians were worried that too many freed Black people were arriving in the Bay State from the South, drawn by its slightly freer society. Should such emigration continue, a legislative committee warned, the dangers included "an indolent, disorderly, and corrupt population," which would gather in the towns. Oh, and these indolent people would also displace many locals from "labors and occupations which, in the end, it would be more advantageous to have performed by the white population of the state." In fact, even as abolitionists like William Lloyd Garrison operated from a Boston stronghold, local racism gathered force; in Minardi's words, "in the decades after the Revolution, the idea of 'race' became a pernicious force throughout the North. . . . Racial ideology reinscribed the inequities of slavery along lines presumed to be natural, as opposed to legal or social." She quotes a preacher, Hosea Easton, of both African and Native descent: "slavery's demise had only fed 'the soul-and-body-destroying energies' of prejudice, a beast 'with all the innate principles of the old dragon himself.'"

ONE SUSPECTS THAT much of that deep prejudice—which, as we shall see, distinguished Massachusetts even in my boyhood— had been there from the start. It's time to raise that other name, Mark Codman, a name I hadn't ever heard back in my tour-guide days. I learned it only because I was rereading Paul Revere's account of his famous midnight ride to Lexington, which contains this passage describing his near apprehension:

I set off upon a very good Horse; it was then about 11 o'Clock, & very pleasant. After I had passed Charlestown Neck, & got nearly opposite where Mark was hung in chains, I saw two men on

Horse back, under a Tree. When I got near them, I discovered they were British officers. One tryed to git a head of Me, & the other to take me. I turned my Horse very quick, & Galloped towards Charlestown neck, and then pushed for the Medford Road. The one who chased me, endeavoring to Cut me off, got into a Clay pond, near where the new Tavern is now built. I got clear of him, and went thro Medford, over the Bridge, & up to Menotomy."

The part of the story that struck me was that phrase "nearly opposite where Mark was hung in chains." Clearly it was a well-known local landmark, since Revere just mentions it casually in passing, but signifying what? Signifying, it turns out, altogether too much. Mark Codman had been enslaved; he and his sister Phillis were owned by a sea captain named John Codman, who was, by all accounts, a brutal master. Brother and sister suffered long enough that, in 1755, they resolved to kill their owner—not to escape slavery, but in order to get "another master." Mark was afraid of sinning; he read his Bible and concluded that if he could kill his tormentor without actually shedding blood he would have avoided the letter of the holy law. He obtained arsenic from a doctor on the pretense he would use it to kill pigs; instead he and his sister poisoned the tea and porridge of John Codman till he died.

He and Phillis were tried and convicted, not just of murder but of petit treason, the first time such a charge had been laid in Massachusetts. Her punishment: she was burned alive. His sentence was almost as grim. After being hanged and then tarred, his body was gibbeted. Do you know about gibbeting? I didn't. It means locked in a human-shaped iron cage and then hung in a public place as a warning—sometimes alive, there to die of starvation, and sometimes, as with Codman, after execution. Gibbeting was fading away in England (among other things, surgeons wanted dead bodies for dissecting), and largely unknown in Massachusetts. But the crime of a Black man murdering his owner was evidently so unsettling that Mark was not only stuck in a cage on a pole—he was left there for decades. By the time Revere rode by him in 1775 he'd been there twenty years; by the time Revere recounted his ride in 1798, more than forty years had passed and yet he still could assume that absolutely everyone would know just what he was talking about. Mark Codman was part of the New England landscape. A landMark.

I'm not completely sure why that story smacked me even harder than the story of Prince Estabrook, but it did. One reason gibbeting was in decline was that contemporary observers complained long and hard about the stink that gibbeted bodies gave off as they decomposed—neighbors had to keep their windows closed for months. The stench still seems pungent to me, scenting everything I like to believe about American history; the line between that iron cage and Derek Chauvin kneeling on George Floyd till he died seems direct, with the same (fearful) need to drive home the reality of everyone's relative place in our society. Revere's ride, immortalized by Longfellow, took him beneath the skeleton of a slave, hung for decades from a pole to remind everyone who was boss. And no one who mattered seemed to have thought a thing of it.

. . . . .

ONCE THE THREAD tugging begins, of course, it continues; that is its nature, and before long your warm and cozy sweater is full of raveling holes.

Consider, briefly, the scholarship that Mary Thompson brought to her 2019 study of George Washington and his slaves. Thompson, a kindred spirit, had started by guiding tourists—sometimes eight thousand a day—at Mount Vernon in 1980. "What that mass audience often wants is an answer to the questions, 'Was George Washington a good slave owner?' or 'He was good to his slaves, wasn't he?'" Yes, well, that is what we white Americans would like. And Thompson—a careful, nuanced historian—makes quite real both the life of those enslaved people and the growing intellectual and moral conflict for Washington, the only one of the Founding Fathers to free his slaves in his will. But her bottom line is clear: "Let me just say upfront that some of the worst things one thinks about in terms of slavery—whipping, keeping someone in shackles, tracking a person down with dogs, or selling people away from their family—all of those things happened at Mount Vernon or on other plantations under Washington's management." As Nikole Hannah-Jones observed in an interview with Ezra Klein of the *Times* in summer 2021, "George Washington wasn't moonlighting as a slave holder. That was their career. That was how they garnered the resources to go off and do these other great things that we so admire and we praise." One of Washington's slaves, by Thompson's account, had taken up with a British prisoner of war held at Mount Vernon during the Revolution, and wanted to return with him to Europe after the British surrender. Washington's overseers said no. "She protested vehemently and in order to insure that she understood she exercised no option in determining her status she was branded with a 'W' on her cheek."

Or consider, again briefly, Ben Franklin, up north in Quaker Philadelphia. We've already seen that, following the custom of the day, he retired at forty-two to become a gentleman, and perhaps no American has ever made better use of that status: aside from his role in discovering electricity, he invented bifocals, improved streetlamps, woodstoves, and odometers, and created the first flexible urinary catheter. (If that last strikes you as unimportant, you are so far lucky.) He helped pioneer the lending library and the fire brigade; he charted the Gulf Stream; he was the first chess player "known by name in the American colonies," and he wrote an essay on the morals of the game still read today. Oh, and his diplomacy in London and Paris was crucial to the outcome of the Revolution. The German philosopher Kant called him "the new Prometheus." But here's the other thing: before he retired, when he was making his fortune editing the *Pennyslvania Gazette*, every single issue carried ads for slaves, or offering rewards for the capture of runaways. "Between one-fifth and one-quarter of the paper's advertisements directly concerned unfree labor," and he often acted as the middleman in the transactions. "Two likely Young Negroes, one a Lad about 19, the Other a Girl of 15, to be Sold. Inquire of the Printer."

One can make excuses. Washington, as Thompson notes, was born into a world where slavery was taken for granted; "he may well have been in his thirties before he ever heard anything critical of slavery." Franklin was eventually a leader in Philadelphia's abolition society. But the point is that this institution—and the racism that accompanied it—was so much a part of American society that there was no escaping it.

The same is true of America's other original sin, the genocidal destruction of the nations that inhabited the continent when Europeans arrived. In fact, no matter where you live in America, you don't need to scratch very deep to find the residue of these crimes. My mother's family, for instance, was from West Virginia. One of the earliest pictures I have of her is from her grade school days in the unincorporated settlement of Yawkey, West Virginia, a tiny hamlet above Charlestown. It was the Depression, and shoes were not in evidence. (The town was named for the Yawkey family, whose scion, Tom, owned the Boston Red Sox for forty-four years; he was a racist—Jackie Robinson called him "one of the most bigoted guys in baseball"—who was the last owner in baseball to integrate his team.) Mom went to high school in Parkersburg, on the other side of West Virginia, and then made the short trip across the Ohio to Marietta for college. Marietta, it turns out, is as good a candidate as any for the first capital of the West—the historian David McCullough uses it as the focus of his study *The Pioneers* about the movement of Americans into the "vast interior," the "howling wilderness." The first of those settler companies arrived from Boston, veterans of the Revolution, and found a land fertile beyond belief: herds of buffalo, hundred-pound pike in the rivers. Within a generation or two they had tamed that land, felling its forests, building towns, funding great public universities. And all it required was moving out the people who were there. McCullough quotes one Wyandot Indian: "No one in particular can justly claim this [land]; it belongs in common to us all; no earthly being has exclusive right to it. The Great Spirit above is the true and only owner of this soil; and He has given us all an equal right to it." That right could not stand up to might; after the defeat of Shawnee chief Blue Jacket by General "Mad Anthony" Wayne at the Battle of Fallen Timbers in 1794, "at Marietta the cloud of fear lifted and life for many returned to the main task of clearing and burning trees." The normalcy of all this—which, like slavery, underpins so much of America's prosperity even to this day—can't be overstated; it was taken for granted in the same way that Revere took Mark's suspended body for granted. It took an outsider—Charles Dickens, visiting on a lecture tour in 1842 during the last stages of "Indian removal"—to actually register the sadness of it all; he described the Native Americans' "strong attachment to the familiar scenes of their infancy, and in particular to the burial-places of their kindred; and of their great reluctance to leave them."

What I'm trying to say is: my life, and the life of other people like me, was built in very real part on the suffering of others. That's not wokeness, and that's not "critical race theory." That's history. And the fact that, to some extent, we've stopped doing these things doesn't mean we get to ignore the effects of earlier actions. As Richard Rothstein observed in his classic account of segregation, *The Color of Law*, "let bygones be bygones" is not a very noble principle if you came out on top.

HAVING SKIPPED BACK in time to 1770, we're going to jump forward two hundred years, returning to the suburb of my youth.

This means sliding past just a few small things in the history of American race relations: the Civil War, Reconstruction, and Jim Crow. But we pick up the story at what seems, initially, a more hopeful time and place: in an increasingly liberal suburb, at the peak of the civil rights movement. Martin Luther King had come to Lexington in 1963—a throng of twelve hundred had jammed the high school auditorium to hear him say that "we have a long long way to go," but that we were "marching to freedom." Two years later, in 1965, there was a cross burning on the lawn of the Catholic church—a crime that went unsolved, though it was apparently in reaction to the fact that the parish priest had gone south to march in Selma. The incident was dramatic, but unrepresentative: its greatest effect, the paper said the next week, had been "to swell the attendance Sunday afternoon at the memorial service on the Battle Green" for the Alabama minister who had been beaten to death during those Southern protests.

Sadly more typical was a small scandal that erupted three years later on Patriot's Day in 1968, when the Boston-based editor of the *Christian Science Monitor* charged in a TV interview that the Lexington police had detained the fourteen-year-old son of one of his Black reporters, an honor student and star football player who had been invited by a white Sunday school classmate to spend the weekend in Lexington. The police report was painfully straightforward: "While assigned to cruiser duty to assist with the control of the crowd gathered to watch the parade, I saw a young fellow in the doorway of the Christian Science Reading Room. My attention was drawn to him as he appeared to be sleeping as he was standing. A closer look revealed" that the zipper to his pants was undone. "I asked him what was wrong, and received no answer, he just smiled and shrugged his shoulders. I then asked him if he were under the influence of drugs and he stated that he was not. I then advised him that his pants were open and he zipped them up." And then the officer took him to the station in the cruiser, and made him take off his shirt so he could search him. "I could see no signs of him having used a needle. He was still acting very vague, as though he was under the influence of something, but I could not detect the odor of alcohol." Finally his white friend arrived at the station and explained that they'd been up late the night before. "Because both boys had the same story and the fact that I was unable to find any narcotics on the suspect's person, I felt that I was perhaps mistaken in my belief that he was under the influence," the policeman wrote. "Although I still feel at this point that he may have been. As for the pants being open, I felt that in the absence of any complaint that this too could be overlooked at this time, as I know where to locate the subject at a later date if necessary." And so a fourteen-year-old boy was not booked for having an unzipped fly.

Predictably, the chief of police said he was "just so damn mad about this," the "this" being the suggestion from the newspaper editor that there was anything untoward in the department's conduct. "I think the boy's mother and father should be glad the officer was concerned and checked to see if he was all right," the chief—the same chief who would soon oversee the mass arrests on the Green—explained. "Whether Negro or White, a man doing something that draws the attention of a policeman should be checked," he added. "You arrest people, you bring them in here for questioning day in and day out and nothing is said. But because this boy has Black skin it makes all the difference." Anyway, the sergeant in question, as the newspaper pointed out, "has cooperated with the Lexington Civil Rights Committee in finding a negro tenant for a house he owns in Lexington." It all faded from view in a matter of weeks, though not, one imagines, from the memory of the fourteen-year-old who was searched for needle marks.

The town's main effort to address the racial turmoil of the era—a response it shared with other liberal suburbs ringing Boston—was a program called METCO, the Metropolitan Council for Educational Opportunity. Early in the 1960s, activists in the city decried the "de facto segregation" of the city's schools; it would be almost a decade before the courts ordered forced busing between Boston's neighborhoods, so in the interim the State House passed a law permitting suburban communities to allow the voluntary enrollment of city kids. (A proposal for local referendums on the plan was defeated perhaps because they feared the kind of embarrassment that would come in a few years with Lexington's vote on public housing.) The first class of 220 kids began riding the bus every morning in 1966, headed for Lexington, Arlington, Braintree, Brookline, Lincoln, Newton, and Wellesley. The program—which continues to this day—has success stories: Audie Cornish, for instance, the host of *All Things Considered*. Or Baltimore city attorney Marilyn Mosby, who got to bring felony charges against six police officers for their role in the death of Freddie Gray in 2015 for possession of a perfectly legal knife. (If it seems like every story leads to another story about the same thing, that should tell you something.)

But METCO was a rough road for the kids involved, who were rising before dawn to take a bus out to a very different world, taking classes all day, perhaps staying for sports practice, and then heading back into the city. Even the successes wondered at the meaning of it all. Mike Mascoll, for instance, started coming to Lexington in the 1970s as a third grader, and he rode the bus from Roxbury right until he graduated from high school, where he led the basketball team to the state championship; he later made a documentary about the program, called *On the Line: Where Sacrifice Begins*. He said he'd learned how to fit into white spaces ("I've been doing it my whole damn life") but as he told an interviewer when the movie came out, the program managed to change his life without having much impact on the world at all. Applying for jobs, he says, "I can't fully put my finger on it, but it still tastes like that whole 'you know, we checked that box, we've got one or two in here. We're good. Thanks but no thanks.'" And if it didn't have much effect on the world at large, it didn't seem to have much effect on the towns involved either. METCO provided "more white folks in the suburbs with an opportunity to kind of have that duality as well, and learn. And the bulk of them missed the boat. They didn't take advantage."

In fact, for some local kids, METCO became an early opportunity to practice resentment. As early as 1969, just three years into the program, a couple of fights led to a walkout of 125 white students who said they feared for their safety. "Whites have no concept of the pressures on black students," the principal said in response. As one of the METCO students explained at the time, they felt "conflicting pressures from their parents, who wanted them to remain in the program, and from their friends, who are opposed to their participation." And the tensions never really waned.

Almost a decade later, for instance, I was supplementing my summer earnings as a tour guide by writing news stories for the local paper, one of a chain of suburban weeklies. Word came that several students across the border in Concord had listed the KKK among their activities in the high school yearbook, and so the newspaper publisher decided that since I was in high school I was the person to "go undercover." He handed me a shirt that he had had printed up that said, "I Hate [N-Word]," on the theory that if I wore it the putative Klansmen would recognize me as a fellow and confess all. (This same publisher would regularly assemble the entire staff and make us watch his print of the Zapruder film of JFK's assassination, assigning us quadrants in case we might notice something the FBI had missed.) I was sixteen, but just smart enough to leave the shirt safely in the trunk of the car; I wandered the poorer section of Concord, away from the mansions along the river, away from Louisa May Alcott's home and Thoreau's grave; eventually I found the kids in question, or at least their friends, over in a neighborhood by the state prison. The consensus was that the Concord Klan was mostly a joke. "They asked me to join," said one, "and they had membership cards and they were going to burn a stake, but it never really got off the ground." Still, there were real racial tensions—mostly, kids said, they were jealous because of what they considered selective enforcement of school rules to avoid confrontation with METCO students. "They are always walking in late to classes, and the teachers never do anything," said one. "They are really afraid of being called racists." Also, "when they are there in the caf, they always play their stereos loud and make a lot of noise," said one girl. "When we do the same thing, they come along and tell us to cut it out. We say what about them and the teachers always say, 'we'll tell them too,' but then they just walk out the door."

As usual, the overt trouble faded. "All the Imperial Wizards graduated," one kid said. "There won't even be talk of a Klan next year." It wasn't like the semi-warfare underway at the same time in the neighborhoods of Boston, where in those years "forced busing" led to stonings, stabbings, a beating of a Black man with an American flag. (It was lost on no one that the court orders were enforced by a judge, W. Arthur Garrity, who lived in Wellesley, another rich suburb and home to one of the original METCO receiving schools.) But, one suspects, the underlying situation in the suburbs remained more or less the same for many years to come: METCO was a useful program that helped some kids and doubtless built some friendships and some understanding as well as some tension and nastiness, all without changing very much about the community. Lexington's population was 1.3 percent African American in 2020, down from 1.5 percent in 2010, down from 3.1 percent in 2000. Boston's public schools, by 2020, were 75 percent Black and Hispanic. Dr. King, back in that 1963 address at Lexington High School, had said the evil of segregated housing was a chief evil; "if we could get rid of it I'm sure there would be progress in other areas." So far, no luck.

LET'S GO BACK in time again to the founding of our country, but just for a little bit: I want to lay the groundwork for thinking about what we need to do right now, at this very late date, if we want to salvage anything from the wreck that is the standard idea of American history. Because let's be real: right now all that talk about equality, and farmers standing up to kings, and so on—the talk that was so appealing to me when I was a guide, and which still stirs me when I read it—is hard to take seriously in a country that has turned out as unequal as the one in which we live.

The attempts to bail out the Founding Fathers seem increasingly lame. Not long ago, for instance, a Republican legislator in Tennessee took to the statehouse floor in an argument over whether schools should teach about institutional racism, to defend the infamous Three-Fifths Compromise in the Constitution that discounted the value of enslaved people compared with their white counterparts. Justin Lafferty, a Knoxville state representative, insisted that "by limiting the population in the count," participants in the Constitutional Convention had "specifically limited the number of representatives that would be available in the slaveholding states, and they did it for the purpose of ending slavery—well before Abraham Lincoln, well before the Civil War." Representative Lafferty added that he had made his remarks without "any malice towards any of my friends on the other side," but simply because he was "exasperated by what he saw as a larger drive," exemplified by the 1619 Project, to "look at the nation's history in a harsher light." In his exasperation, he echoed Dr. King, who once explained, "There comes a time when people get tired. We are here this evening to say to those who have mistreated us so long that we are tired—tired of being segregated and humiliated; tired of being kicked about by the brutal feet of oppression." In a similar vein, Representative Lafferty explained that he had made his remarks "only because I'm tired, y'all. The people of this nation are tired." Ah, the wearying

work of standing up for racist history—it's almost like what Rosa
Parks went through.

His argument is, of course, ridiculous. If the members of the
Constitutional Convention had wanted to get rid of slavery they
could have, then and there, as indeed the Northern states did in
their state charters. But they didn't because—well, because the
predecessors of men like Representative Lafferty made clear they
wouldn't sign on if they did. The only excuse you can begin to
make for the founders of the new nation, it seems to me, is that
slave owners held enough power that they were able to force
everyone else to go along, at the cost of preventing America from
being born if they didn't get their way. This seems to have been
the calculation the Northerners made from the start. Consider, for
instance, the 1776 convention in Philadelphia, the one that wrote
the Declaration of Independence. As it met, the British troops
had just evacuated Boston, and their warships roamed the coast—
against that backdrop, historian George Daughan writes, the
Massachusetts delegation let their counterparts in the Carolinas,
worried by "the first stirrings of an antislavery movement in New
England," know they wouldn't be raising the issue: "Doing something about human bondage in America would require redoing
the whole of society, particularly in the South. And it would mean
the end of a unified Congress. Massachusetts would be left to its
fate. Members were determined not to let that happen, and quietly
gave big slave owners a significant victory." Even back home in
Massachusetts, where a group of slaves petitioned the Provincial
Congress in 1775 to end human bondage in the colony, leaders
like Hancock decided it was "not the time," because "the unity of
the Continental Congress" could have been undermined. A dozen

years later, when the moment came to write the Constitution, the time still had not come; all the Revolutionary rhetoric about not wanting to be enslaved by the British was seemingly forgotten. If, privately, Washington confided to Jefferson he'd move north if the nation split, he wasn't ready to force that division. No one was ready—the South called everyone's bluff, if a bluff it was. The secretary of the Pennsylvania Abolition Society asked Franklin, its putative president, to present a petition to Congress; Franklin demurred, suggesting that it be left to "lie over for the present."

I'm not saying these were good bargains. It's quite possible to argue that, given the hideous reality of slavery, moral colonists should have stayed as loyal subjects of the British Empire, which moved more quickly to abolish human bondage within its realm. Or that they should have forced the debate between North and South then and there, instead of letting it "lie over for the present." What I'm saying is, if you read the history to mean that the Founding Fathers had no choice, then you have no choice: you have to figure out how to make good, even at this remove, their fateful bargain.

There have been times in our history when we thought we were on the verge of doing just that. The Civil War resulted from that bargain, and it killed more people than any conflict in our history—in fact, it killed roughly the same number as all our other wars combined. But the victory was squandered when politicians—of the type, I would imagine, now represented by Tennessee representative Justin Lafferty—managed to quash Reconstruction and handed control of the South, and the lives of its Black residents, back to the same kind of men who had won the bluff in Philadelphia. It seemed as if we might have been on the verge of making good that bargain in the 1960s, when the civil rights movement brought an end to Jim Crow. But then communities like, say, Lexington voted against subsidized housing, substituting palliatives like METCO; in the Northeast, the percentage of Black students in schools that are 90 to 100 percent minority has steadily risen since 1970. Sixty-two percent of Black kids born between 1955 and 1970 grew up in neighborhoods of high or medium poverty. For Black kids born since 1970, that number has grown to 66 percent. Whatever momentum we might have thought was building in the wake of the King years petered out, and the old ugly tide washed back in, with the drug war and mass incarceration and the "end of welfare as we know it."

So—what do we do now, in the early years of the 2020s, if we have some desire to make good that ugly bargain? If we have some remaining stake in the idea that the American experiment had something noble about it? (Or even if we've given up on American history and just want something that resembles justice?)

ONE THING WE should do is decide, in as many places as possible, to reverse Thing Two, the decision that Lexington—and so many other suburbs—made to bar apartment developments. Because it turns out that this is perhaps the single most effective example of what people now call "structural racism." (Which seems a polite way of putting it—it's "structural" in that it's built into the system, but structures don't build themselves. Particular people went to the polls on a particular day and made a particular choice.) A town like Lexington is 1.3 percent Black in large part because its zoning mostly prevents multifamily housing, in favor of everyone having a house like the one I grew up in, with its own driveway, its own tree, its own backyard. Since that makes things more expensive, it severely limits who ends up there. Even among the top 10 percent of Americans, who are the only ones likely to afford to live in a high-end suburb, the net worth of white families is $1,786,000, versus $343,160 for Black families.

We know the importance of multifamily housing because of common sense, but also because of data. Matthew Resseger is an economist with Boston's planning authority—he got his PhD from Harvard in 2014, where he wrote a dissertation trying to answer the question of whether "local zoning regulations such as minimum lot size requirements and restrictions on the permitting of multifamily housing may exacerbate racial segregation by reducing in some neighborhoods the construction of units that appeal to prospective minority residents." This seems intuitive—if you build a bunch of homes at once, sharing walls and driveways and yards, you can sell them for less, and cheaper housing should allow people with less money to move in. But it's hard to aggregate the data—dozens of suburbs orbit every city, each with their own laws. Resseger focused on Massachusetts, looking at small areas that crossed zoning boundaries—or, as he put it, "variation in block-level racial composition within narrow bands around zone borders within jurisdictions." And what he found was "robust evidence that land use regulation does negatively impact minority population shares on more restrictively zoned blocks." If you increased the allowable density by ten dwelling units per acre, you'd increase "the block's Black share by 3.8 percentage points and the Hispanic share by 5 percentage points, roughly doubling the base share for both groups." The same thing happens when you permit multifamily housing. And the effect has grown stronger, not weaker, since 1990. The Boston metro area is one of the most tightly zoned metro areas in the country, which is why it remains highly segregated; metro areas like Houston, Dallas, or Oklahoma City, with less restrictive zoning, are far more integrated. "As much as three quarters of the Boston to Houston gap could be accounted for by land use regulation alone," Resseger found.

Remember Nikole Hannah-Jones? Before she went to the *New York Times* where she oversaw the 1619 Project, she was working at ProPublica, the independent nonprofit investigative journalism project. And there she conducted a remarkable probe of this precise issue, this time in the affluent suburbs of New York City. Towns like Scarsdale and White Plains adopted zoning codes in the 1920s aimed at keeping out lower-cost housing, and they were followed by every other suburb in Westchester County, which trails only Manhattan in median income among New York counties. On average, Westchester's affluent suburbs—Chappaqua or Rye, say—set aside less than 2 percent of their acreage for apartments or condos; the county's much poorer small cities, places like Port Chester or Mount Vernon, zone six times more of their land for multifamily housing, and as a result are far more diverse. The county's fair housing plan, adopted in 1993, called for five thousand new affordable housing units countywide within a decade, but the twelve whitest towns "did not add a single unit of affordable housing during those years." Eventually, under a federal court order, the county agreed to build 750 units of affordable housing within seven years in its thirty-two whitest jurisdictions, and to market that housing to Black and Latino residents across the New York area.

And then what happened? Three months later, the Westchester county executive who had signed that deal was defeated in his reelection bid, taken down by a radio station owner named Rob Astorino in one of the "most stunning upsets" in local political history. The new county executive—the region's most important political figure—told local officials that he would "not force anyone to build anything." To comply with the letter of the legal settlement, the county announced plans to build the new apartments on tiny slivers of land right next to the boundaries of the diverse cities—the eighteen units slated for Rye, the thirtieth wealthiest town in America, were slated for a slice of land physically separated from the town by Interstates 287 and 95. In Cortlandt, "officials proposed a development on a strip of land . . . wedged along a highway and a railroad track. The site met the criteria for low concentrations of African Americans and Latinos only because, other than the residents of the nursing home, two homeless shelters and a psychiatric hospital nearby, no one lived on that land." In Chappaqua, where Bill and Hillary Clinton live, and which in 2008 CNN had listed as fifth on their list of "top-earning towns," the county proposed to build the affordable housing in "a non-residential part of Chappaqua crammed between railroad tracks and a highway."

County leader Astorino was entirely unapologetic—indeed, when the Obama administration put forth a new anti-discrimination rule in 2013 called "Affirmatively Furthering

Fair Housing" or AFFH, he took to the pages of the *Wall Street Journal* to call it an "assault on local zoning." Under the new rules, he wrote, "apartments, high rises, or whatever else the federal government wants can be built on any block in America." Donald Trump suspended enforcement of the new housing rules on taking office—not surprising, perhaps, for a man whose real-estate developer father had marched with the Klan, and whose entry into public life was helping settle a housing discrimination lawsuit with the federal government. (Among other remedies, the court ordered young Donald and his fellow executives to "thoroughly acquaint themselves personally on a detailed basis" with the fair housing laws.) But it was only during the 2020 campaign, when he found himself trailing Biden in the polls, that Trump started stressing the issue. "At the request of many great Americans who live in the Suburbs, and others, I am studying the AFFH housing regulation that is having a devastating impact on these once thriving suburban areas," he tweeted. "Not fair to homeowners, I may END!" Hours later, his son—the grandson of the Klansman—posted a link to an article in the right-wing *National Review* titled "Joe Biden and Dems Are Set to Abolish the Suburbs." Allowing multifamily housing, the magazine explained, would mean "the end of local control, the end of a style of living that many people prefer to the city, and therefore the end of meaningful choice in how Americans can live.

"Since the Pilgrims first landed," it continued, "our story has been of a people who chose how and where to live." True enough—ask the original inhabitants. But of course not all

Americans could choose where to live, and Trump clearly wanted to keep it that way. Campaigning in Michigan, he asked voters, "Would you like a nice low-income housing project next to your suburban, beautiful, ranch-style house?" In Wisconsin he upped the fear factor a little more: Biden will "eliminate single-family zoning, bringing who knows into your suburbs, so your communities will be unsafe and your housing values will go down." He sounded imploring, almost desperate: "Suburban women, will you please like me? I saved your damn neighborhood, OK?"

White women did, as a group, vote for Trump (though not as heavily as white men). But it wasn't quite enough for him to carry the election. And so the Biden administration reinstated the AFFH rule. And now we're back where we were in the 1960s, at the dawn of the fair housing laws. Except a town like Lexington is even less Black than it was then.

MOST LIKELY IT will remain so. Because over those many decades of suburban prosperity and suburban discrimination, affluent white Americans have built such a massive lead in wealth that they, in effect, control the game: their victory has been, as it were, locked in, and it will take far more than fair housing laws to level things out.

To put this in easy to understand terms: my parents bought their house on Middle Street in 1970 for $30,000, which would be the rough equivalent of $205,000 in today's dollars. But in fact, if you go on the real estate website Zillow and take a look, the house is actually now worth an estimated $987,000. That $800,000 over inflation is the premium that came from getting in near the ground floor and riding the suburbs up. The affluent American suburb may be the greatest wealth accumulation engine of all time—at least until the financial crisis of 2008, a surefire guaranteed ride. But you had to be able to buy a ticket at the start: you needed that $30,000, or access to a bank that would lend it to you. If you had that, let the compounding begin; if you didn't, then you could stand on the sidelines and watch your relative position erode.

And of course what American history meant was that Black people didn't have, by and large, the chance to buy that ticket. Because they'd worked for free as slaves for hundreds of years, with no chance of building up family wealth. Because after Reconstruction came to its premature end, they were re-subjugated in systems like sharecropping that might as well have been slavery (in the 1930s, many sharecroppers were earning the equivalent of ten cents a day). Because the New Deal programs systematically cut out Black Americans: when Social Security came into effect, farmers and domestic workers were the two classes of employees excluded, which meant 65 percent of Black Americans didn't benefit (and that meant that, in addition to everything else, the children of those maids and farmers would have to support their parents as they aged in ways their white peers didn't, adding to the economic burden). When a million Black Americans went off to the Second World War, they were the theoretical beneficiaries of the GI Bill on their return—but often they weren't allowed to attend the colleges that were boosting the education and hence the earnings of white former servicemen. And as we have seen, they were systematically prevented from getting the bank loans that would have let them buy into the suburbs at the very start. Indeed, realtors worked to panic white city dwellers—they'd hire Black people to stroll the streets, and then begin cold-calling homeowners, offering lowball prices with the warning that the homes would soon be worth nothing. This "blockbusting" worked, and once the white residents had fled, the homes were sold or rented at exorbitant prices to Black families who had no other place to go. When those Black families tried to move to white areas, they were often driven out. Ta-Nehisi Coates tells the story of the first Black family to move into the ur-suburb of Levittown, Pennyslvania, in the 1940s: Daisy and Bill Myers were "greeted with protests and a burning cross." And the salient point is that their neighbors understood *exactly* the economic stakes. A neighbor who joined in the protests told reporters that Bill Myers was "probably a nice guy, but every time I look at him I see $2,000 drop off the value of my house."

It's actually not that hard to put a cash value on all this endless sad history. You can do it piecemeal—the exclusion of Black farmers and domestic workers from Social Security accounts for a loss of 150 billion dollars of wealth in today's currency. Or you can do it from the other end, and simply ask yourself: how much money do white families have, and how much do Black families have? Unless you're a racist who thinks that there's some difference between groups in intelligence or ability, that number is the bottom-line derivation of history, oppression transmuted into dollars. And the numbers are almost unbelievably stark: in 2014, for every dollar in a white household, a Black household had *less than seven cents.*

The wealth gap hasn't gone down in the years since the

civil rights movement; it's gone up, and steadily. And it keeps compounding—if you have less capital, for instance, you have to take out more college loans, keeping you deeper in debt for decades. White families, by contrast, are five times more likely than Black families to receive large bequests. And, again, suburbs like Lexington are the biggest driving force in broadening this gap, because that's where so much wealth accumulated.

Dorothy Brown, a professor at Emory University, published a book in 2021 called *The Whiteness of Wealth* that examines the numbers in painful detail. Between 1940 and 1950, as suburbanization began, a majority of white Americans became homeowners "by riding a wave of anti-Black policies—public and private—that prevented Black families from buying in certain neighborhoods and from taking advantage of FHA-insured loans. By the end of the 1950s, 98 percent of homes built with FHA support after World War II were occupied by white Americans." Meanwhile, Black Americans were confined to areas that saw none of the big gains in housing prices—indeed, the value of the homes in those neighborhoods often fell, because of the quality of the services available, and because white people—statistically—didn't want to move there, depressing the size of the possible demand. And what do you know—beginning in 1951, people were allowed to sell their houses and take up to $500,000 in capital gains tax free. Only 44 percent of Black families own homes anyway, compared with three-quarters of white Americans—which means the latter get an array of benefits from the government, like a mortgage interest deduction.

That house on Middle Street was built in 1950. The money

my mother took out of it—tax free—when she sold it after my father's death is what allowed her to move into a comfortable retirement community, which kept her safe during COVID. And it's what allows me and my brother not to be paying for her support as she ages, so we can in turn pass more money on to our kids. That this is clearly unfair does *not* mean that my parents didn't work hard their whole lives—they did. It doesn't mean my brother and I haven't worked hard—we have, and so have our kids. But it does mean that we got an unearned boost the whole time: the economic wind was at our backs, the gravity of money was tugging in our direction. And others, because of the color of their skin, faced an unrelenting headwind. Economic gravity kept pulling them down. The wealth gap widened even during the pandemic, but of course the wealth gap was the least of it. Black people were twice as likely to die of COVID, which is the bottom-est of bottom lines.

ALL THIS IS a prelude to saying: it is long past time to actually talk about reparations. Long, long past time.

To return for a second to colonial Boston: in 1773, after Crispus Attucks was killed in the Boston Massacre, but before Prince Estabrook was shot on Lexington Green, a committee speaking "on behalf of our fellow slaves" asked the colony's legislature for their freedom. "We are very sensible that it would be highly detrimental to our present masters, if we were allowed to demand all that of right belongs to us for past services; this we disclaim." Given their position of no strength at all—given that the body of

a slave was hanging in an iron cage nearby—that was savvy nego-
tiating: "Forget what we're owed, we'll settle for our freedom."
But it obviously wasn't fair—not then, and not two hundred and
fifty years later when even that nominal freedom, granted by the
state in 1780, proved to be a series of traps.

In fact, it was only a few years later—1783—when a formerly
enslaved woman, Belinda Royall, presented a petition to the
Massachusetts General Assembly requesting a pension from the
proceeds of her former master's estate. Her words are remarkable:
she describes her girlhood along the Volta River in what today
would be Ghana. "The mountains covered with spicy forests, the
valleys loaded with the richest fruits, spontaneously produced;
joined to that happy temperature of air," a happiness complete
until "in a sacred grove, with each hand in that of a tender Par-
ent, she was paying her devotions to the great Orisa who made
all things [when] an armed band of white men, driving many of
her Countrymen in Chains, ran into the hallowed shade!" She
describes for the legislators her voyage to America, with "three
hundred Affricans in chains, suffering the most excruciating tor-
ments; and some of them rejoicing, that the pangs of death came
like a balm to their wounds." And she describes how, for fifty
years, "though she was a free moral agent, accountable for her
actions, yet she never had a moment at her own disposal!" And
then she makes her claim: "The face of your Petitioner, is now
marked with the furrows of time, and her frame feebly bending under the oppression of years, while she, by the Laws of the
Land, is denied the enjoyment of one morsel of that immense
wealth, apart whereof hath been accumulated by her own indus-

try." Therefore, she asks "that such allowance may be made her out of the estate of Colonel Royall, as will prevent her and her more infirm daughter from misery in the greatest extreme, and scatter comfort over the short and downward path of their Lives." And indeed it was—but only 15 pounds and 12 shillings for her lifetime's labor, and even that was granted, as far as historians can tell, only because Colonel Royall had been a loyalist who fled Massachusetts for the safety of Nova Scotia, leaving his estate behind.

In any event, the judgment failed to establish a precedent, and for most of the centuries that followed no one got a thing. Not—once Reconstruction was abandoned—the forty acres and a mule that had been promised. Not when Callie House, in 1898, formed the National Ex-Slave Mutual Relief, Bounty and Pension Association, which grew to hundreds of thousands of members. Not when Marcus Garvey made the call in the 1920s, nor when Harlem's Queen Mother Audley Moore presented a petition to the United Nations in 1959. Not in 1988, when reparations—a $20,000 check and an apology—were given to the Japanese Americans interned during World War II. Not when Randall Robinson published his book *The Debt* in 2000 (though it was a best seller), nor when Coates issued his treatise in 2014 (though it may have been the most widely read piece of political journalism of the era). Every year since 1989, H.R. 40—deriving its name from those post–Civil War acres that never came—has been introduced in Congress, asking merely for a commission to study the possibility of reparations. It has yet to even be voted on.

Still, there are at least a few signs that the day of recompense draws nearer—state legislatures and city councils have passed resolutions in support of reparations. And in the spring of 2021, the city of Evanston, just outside Chicago and home to Northwestern University, voted to take the money it earned from marijuana sales and dedicate it to a fund for reparations, granting qualifying households up to $25,000 for home repairs or down payments. The plan reflects, its authors said, both the disproportionate prosecutions of Black people for drug possession, and the "harm caused by discriminatory housing policies and practices." The legislation followed a report on the city's history, which put things plainly: "While the policies, practices, and patterns may have evolved over the course of these generations, their impact was cumulative and permanent," the authors wrote. "They were the means by which legacies were limited and denied." The first payments went out in the spring, and the Reverend Michael Nabors, a local NAACP chapter president who leads Evanston's Second Baptist Church, called it the most exciting time in his sixty-one years. "It is Evanston today and, in my opinion, it is going to be the United States tomorrow," he said. "We are leading the way."

If that movement is to stretch beyond a few college towns, however, it will require Americans across the great suburban expanse to reckon with the fact that money is how we measure things. Lexington made its Good Neighbor pledge in 1962: "I will accept families and individuals into my neighborhood without discrimination because of religion, color, or national origin." But the words were empty because they didn't come with cash attached; people were unwilling to pay up. When people tried to attach cash to them—Thing Two, that town-wide referendum on affordable housing, which might have temporarily dropped property values a little—the effort went down in a landslide.

IF, IN 1970, words were as far as people were prepared to go when it came to race, some of that was perhaps understandable. The civil rights movement, at its start, had been framed as a series of political, not economic, changes: the right to ride a bus, the right to sit at a diner, the right to cast a vote. It had been about removing the barriers to citizenship—about giving Black Americans all the rights everyone else enjoyed. When Martin Luther King spoke to that overflow crowd at Lexington High School in 1963, he told the stories he usually told in his stump speech—about Southern county clerks, for instance, who asked Black people trying to register to vote impossible questions: "How many bubbles are there in a bar of soap?" He said that segregation was on the defensive everywhere, and indeed that only three American states remained largely unintegrated—South Carolina, Alabama, and "the great sovereign state of Mississippi." America, he said, had "come a long long way. Speaking figuratively in Biblical language we have broken loose from the Egypt of slavery. We have moved through the wilderness of segregation, and we stand on the border of the promised land of integration. And there can be no gainsaying the fact that old man segregation is on his deathbed, and the only thing uncertain about it is how costly the nation will make the funeral." The crowd roared, and I am sure they meant it—had there been a segregated lunch counter in town, I have no doubt that as many townspeople who went to jail for the Vietnam Veterans Against the War would have done the same for the Southern Christian Leadership Conference.

But perhaps 1963 was the high point of that strand of the civil rights movement. The March on Washington and King's Dream speech were just five months after his Lexington appearance, and in that epic speech from the steps of the Lincoln Memorial, King introduced that concept of a "promissory note" to which "every American was to fall heir. This note was a promise that all men ... would be guaranteed the unalienable rights of life, liberty, and the pursuit of happiness," he said.

> It is obvious today that America has defaulted on this promissory note insofar as her citizens of color are concerned. Instead of honoring this sacred obligation, America has given the Negro people a bad check, a check which has come back marked insufficient funds. But we refuse to believe that the bank of justice is bankrupt. We refuse to believe that there are insufficient funds in the great vaults of opportunity of this nation. And so we have come to cash this check, a check that will give us upon demand the riches of freedom and the security of justice.

His language was still symbolic—that promissory note was a promise that all Americans "would be guaranteed the unalienable rights of life, liberty, and the pursuit of happiness." But as the 1960s wore on, the nature of that demand changed. The check, more and more, became a real instrument in King's mind, to be paid in actual cash.

Peniel Joseph, a University of Texas historian, recently published a remarkable joint biography of Dr. King and Malcolm X,

The Sword and the Shield. It argued that a series of events—the rise of Malcolm's (and then Stokely Carmichael's) campaigns for Black dignity and power, and the economic oppression revealed in the ashes of the riots in places like Watts—transformed King's message over the last half decade of his life. Perhaps King's "most enduring legacy," according to Joseph, "is the commitment to and introduction of what I call *radical black citizenship*. . . . After the urban rebellion of Watts, King came to realize that in addition to voting, true citizenship included a good job, living wage, decent housing, quality education, health care, and nourishment." King had spent most of his life fighting *against* segregation, but it was becoming clear he'd need to fight *for* real equality. The signs were subtle at first: in 1964, in Oslo to accept the Nobel Peace Prize, he said, "We feel we have much to learn from Scandinavia's democratic socialist tradition and from the manner in which you have overcome many of the social and economic problems that still plague a far more powerful and affluent nation." By the Detroit riots of 1967 he was calling for "the creation of a national agency that shall provide a job to every person who needs work." And in 1968, of course, he launched the Poor People's Campaign, whose "ultimate goal" would be to "drive the nation to a guaranteed annual income."

In the spring of that year, he was crisscrossing the country, trying to raise support for what he hoped would be a massive, multiracial march from Mississippi to the nation's capital. "We ought to come in mule carts, in old trucks, any kind of transportation people can get their hands on. People ought to come to Washington, sit down if necessary in the middle of the street and say, 'We are here; we are poor; we don't have any money; you have made us this way . . . and we've come to stay until you do something about it.'"

It was hard going; white politicians who had been happy to decry segregation were less happy with this new message. But Bobby Kennedy did offer his support—protesters needed to come to DC to "make hunger and poverty visible since the country's attention had turned to the Vietnam War and put poverty and hunger on the back burner," he said. And King was committed. In fact, his trips to Memphis that spring, in support of Black garbagemen striking for a living wage, were a kind of test case. The strikers, he said, were reminding America that "it is a crime for people to live in this rich nation and receive starvation wages." On the night of April 3, he took to the pulpit at the Mason Temple in Memphis and preached his final sermon.

It's all right to talk about "long white robes over yonder," in all of its symbolism. But ultimately people want some suits and dresses and shoes to wear down here. It's all right to talk about "streets flowing with milk and honey," but God has commanded us to be concerned about the slums down here, and his children who can't eat three square meals a day. It's all right to talk about the new Jerusalem, but one day, God's preachers must talk about the new New York, the new Atlanta, the new Philadelphia, the new Los Angeles, the new Memphis, Tennessee. This is what we have to do.

The next day he was shot and killed, and Bobby Kennedy soon thereafter. And that was the effective end for a very long time to talk about changing the way our world worked. Who knows if history would have been different had they lived—a formidable backlash was already building, and we went in a very different direction as a nation. It's only now—in the days of Black Lives Matter and the Green New Deal, as the Biden administration strives to pass massive jobs bills and reduce the levels of inequality—that there's some sense of return to 1968. Now, as then, the suburbs will be crucial to how it all plays out.

If one wanted to indict places like Lexington in those years, it's easy: their residents were fine with the concept of civil rights and inclusion and being a good neighbor as long as it required no actual sacrifice. "We waited too long to try to undo [segregation]," economic historian Richard Rothstein writes. "By the time labor market discrimination abated sufficiently for substantial numbers of African Americans to reach the middle class, homes outside urban Black neighborhoods had mostly become unaffordable for working and lower-middle-class families." In fact, all the liberal pledges of goodwill in places like Lexington must have sounded more like taunts. There was a "Welcome" sign at the inn, but "No Vacancy" flashed as well.

If one wanted to offer an excuse for places like Lexington in those years, it might go something like this: the nation had been through enormous change and upheaval in the 1960s, and people needed to take a breath, just as after the Revolution there came a period of consolidation, of adjusting to change. I mean, we went to the moon in those years, and then we pretty much stopped. Perhaps societies get tired like people do, and need a rest. But that's an easier excuse to make if you weren't the one who got to suffer for the next five decades—the one jailed, the one deprived of a good education, the one left to languish in debt. And in any event, this lame excuse for an excuse only makes sense if, *now*, we seize the moment we're in and finally make change real, which will be hard. As Rothstein writes, "moving from an urban apartment to a suburban home is incomparably more difficult than registering to vote, applying for a job, or changing seats on a bus."

I'm not sure what form reparations should take, and it's not my call in any event. Perhaps steps like Biden's child tax credits are a first small down payment on that debt, even if they go to all parents below a certain income. There are dozens of other sound ideas—the National African American Reparations Commission offers ten, beginning with an apology and including free tuition at historically Black colleges for students "committed to providing services to Black communities," as well as "grants and loans for people seeking affordable housing." The National Coalition of Blacks for Reparations in America—with chapters across the country and throughout the African diaspora—pushes hard for HR 40, setting up a congressional committee not just to study the legacy of slavery and segregation, but also to "examine the post–Jim Crow period and the current laws that continue to this day."

I don't underestimate the political difficulty involved—there's no idea that repels the Right as much, and probably much of the middle too. A 2021 poll found only 28 percent of white Americans supported reparations, with 90 percent of Republicans opposed. As a conservative pundit put it on Tucker Carlson's TV show, it's time for African Americans to "move on." "Yeah," replied Carlson: reparations are "really divisive." Surely some of the hysteria over "critical race theory" is just a preemptive strike against the idea of financial justice. (In Oklahoma, for instance, the governor signed a law banning the teaching of such ideas in schools: teachers must not instruct students that "an individual, by virtue of his or her race or sex, bears responsibility for actions committed in the past by other members of the same race or sex," nor make students feel "guilt" or "anguish.") It's an effort, I think, to make sure that this justice window closes like the ones before it, and the idea of reparations is radioactive enough that it may succeed.

Rothstein offers some examples of possible "remedies," a term he prefers to reparations. The federal government could buy the next 15 percent of houses that go up for sale in the suburbs at the market rate, and then sell to Black Americans for the price their grandparents would have paid—the equivalent of that $30,000 my parents invested. "Of course no presently constituted Congress would adopt such a policy," he writes, and of course he's right. But what unalarming, inexpensive tool do you propose to break this chain of history? Again, it's not wokeness. It's math. Black Americans have seven cents on the white dollar. History begets arithmetic. Begets reality.

What can one do but press hard and see what happens? I'm aware that for some all this speculation already comes too late—that too much time has passed, and too much injustice, and that the idea of America is irredeemably stained. Ta-Nehisi Coates wrote of this at the end of his classic book *Between the World and Me* that America's racism runs so deep that only an environmental apocalypse could dent our civilization enough to root it out. He may be right. And of course we may find out.

MY SCOUT TROOP got to raise the flag over Lexington Green at dawn on the Bicentennial celebration of the first battle of the Revolution. We practiced a lot the week before, unfolding the flag from its tight triangle and hooking up the halyards—I spent some nights contemplating what would happen if we used the wrong set of grommets and raised the flag upside down. And I felt a real swell of patriotism that morning, a swell that has dramatically diminished in the years since.

But the flag means only what the country means, and maybe that meaning can change: we get the chance to shape some of what our history stands for with our actions now. If we work for real justice in the 2020s—with deep steps like paying reparations—then the history that began on Lexington Green looks more like the start of something in which we can have a limited but real pride. It's odd to say that we can make our history better, since it's obviously already happened. And we can't, of course, do anything about those who came before us, or remake the events of our own lives; our only possibility for action comes in what's left of our own lifetimes. What we choose to do will help us figure out whether "all men are created equal" was an awkward lie or a promise that took much too long to fulfill.

Many of us who were alive in 1970 are alive still, and we have the resources and political power, if we want to use them, to take history off rewind and put it again in forward motion. If we do so, then perhaps we will eventually earn the right to raise the flag once more with the conviction that it carries some of the meaning that we'd once, naively, taken for granted.

THE CROSS

. . . .

There are few areas of bipartisan agreement in our riven political world, but one of them is that the song "Kumbaya" is a joke. During a single week in the 2012 presidential campaign, for instance, Republican presidential candidate Rick Perry said, "If you're looking for somebody that's going to say, 'Hey, listen, we're not going to make it hard on you, it's all going to work it out, and it's just, you know, "Kumbaya,"' I'm not your guy." Perennial right-wing presidential candidate Rick Santorum, chimed in, decrying national service programs: "Someone's going to pick up trash in a park and sing 'Kumbaya' around a campfire.... That's not what America is all about." The late Herman Cain: Singing "Kumbaya" "is not a foreign policy strategy." And that same week Obama press secretary Jay Carney had this to say: "I don't think that anybody expected or expects Washington to be a campfire where everybody holds hands together and sings 'Kumbaya.' That's not what the nation's business is about." Obama himself, on the complexities of Middle East peace: "This can't be reduced to a matter of somehow let's all, you know, hold hands and sing 'Kumbaya.'" And so on, ad infinitum. As the essayist Michael Ross observed, "Derision of the song and its emotional foundation has become a required sign of toughness and pragmatism in American politics today."

I've paid attention to this trend over the years because I actually grew up singing "Kumbaya," sometimes around a campfire, always earnestly. It was a staple of my church youth group, an organization that did much to shape my life. And it wasn't just "Kumbaya": also "Lord of the Dance," "He's Got the Whole World in His Hands," "Day by Day" (indeed anything from *Godspell*), and "Morning Has Broken." Was there always a girl with a guitar, fussing with a capo and then breaking into song? There was. (Was she always beautiful, an icon of sophistication? In my memory, yes.) In the Fellowship Hall, where we held confirmation class; in the upstairs room, where the high school youth group met on Sunday nights; on the beach at the Cape Cod retreat center that the church conference maintained; at the parties in someone's rec room, where a Cat Stevens album was likely on the turntable. Heck, we sang "Put Your Hand in the Hand." And we did it without much irony. I didn't know then the story behind "Kumbaya"—I thought it was African, but that was only sort of right; it actually comes from the Gullah culture of Georgia's Sea Islands. But we all knew that it meant "come by here," a plea directed at God. We could feel the weight of sadness and hope it contained. And we took it seriously. "Someone's crying, Lord, kumbaya."

I'm going to try something in this chapter that I'm not sure I can pull off, which is to come to grips with what happened to American Christianity in my lifetime. No single change in our culture during my life (save perhaps for the rise of the internet and social media) has meant more, I think, than the loss of mainstream Christianity's power and authority in American life; we've gone from a place where it was central to our identity to a place where, especially in suburban and liberal circles, it's marginal. More than marginal: disparaged or, more commonly, disregarded. There are reasons for this, many of them good; the decline of mainline American Christianity came with real pluses. But there were also costs: for instance, that the idea we could hold hands and sing a song together is now a joke. It's a story intertwined with the other stories I'm telling—about race, about carbon, about prosperity. And I'm not sure they can be understood without it.

In my case, it's mostly a white story, though with a very important Black character. The Black church has its own remarkable history (beautifully recounted by the historian Henry Louis Gates last year, both on television and in print); if that church is dealing with some declines and stresses of its own, it remains a more stable and fundamental part of community and political life. At any rate, it's not my story to recount: the church I knew growing up, like the town it sat so comfortably in, was overwhelmingly white.

THIS BEING LEXINGTON, we begin with some history. Richard Kollen, the most determined chronicler of the town's religious history, notes that it became a town in the late seventeenth century precisely because, as more people settled there, it became impractical for them to travel all the way back to Cambridge (eight miles!) for Sunday services. "The settlers were relieved of the portion of their tax obligation that supported the Cambridge church and were permitted to collect funds to support their own minister. Records of public meetings during this time show business to be concerned almost exclusively with raising funds to build a church and settle a minister." A town in Puritan Massachusetts was precisely the collection of people who belonged to a church. As long as they belonged to the Cambridge church, the growing population of Lexington "could not lay out roads or control their school." So they were very pleased to finish their meetinghouse (though it was "a rude structure even by seventeenth-century standards ... unpainted and with a shingle roof"), and to hire their first minister, Benjamin Estabrook, whose family would later enslave Prince.

Reverend Estabrook died within a year of his first sermon in the new meetinghouse, but that was the end of religious turmoil for a very long time, since his two successors between them filled the pulpit for the next 105 years. The first, John Hancock, preached for 54 years; as we've seen, he was the grandfather of the man who scrawled his name across the Declaration of Independence. Reverend Hancock was so beloved that he was called Bishop, though of course these Congregational churches, so jealous of their independence, had no actual ecclesial hierarchy. His prestige, and his political savvy, meant that the town made it through the revival years of the Great Awakening without the schisms that rent other communities; instead, the steady course of religious life in Lexington remained largely unchanged throughout the eighteenth century. Sunday was the only day of the week when work ceased; everyone in town came to church, and church lasted all day, with a noon break for lunch that was the main social occasion of the week. (It was no accident that the tavern was directly across the road from the church; indeed state law required it.) Sermons stretched on—there was an hourglass near the front of the sanctuary, and congregations felt cheated if it wasn't turned at least once during the talk. (The deacons also had a long pole, with a brass ball on one end and a feather on the other—if a woman or child fell asleep, they were tickled; men were bonked.) As the town grew, the church did as well: a second-floor gallery was added in 1722 to seat the enslaved and the poor; meanwhile, committees occasionally reassigned the seats on the ground floor to reflect the shifting public standing of residents—fines were levied for sitting in the wrong pew.

But if that makes the church sound conservative, it also became a bastion of resistance to colonial authority. When Reverend Hancock died in midcentury, he was succeeded by a twenty-five-year-old Harvard graduate (Harvard having been founded to train Congregational ministers) named Jonas Clarke, who would be the town's foremost citizen until his death in 1805. Clarke and his wife, Lucy (a cousin of John Hancock), had twelve children who survived infancy. He farmed his land to supplement his income, but he also traveled constantly across the colony, filling the pulpits of other pastors (which conveniently let him use the same sermon more than once), attending ordinations, and trading political gossip. One British official in Boston referred to a "black regiment," by which he meant the clergy in their dark coats. ("The Town of Boston being a Metropolis, it was also the Metropolis of Sedition; and hence it was that their Clergy being dependent on the People for their daily Bread; by having frequent Intercourse with the People, imbibed their Principles.") And the Brits were right to worry. Since New England churchgoers, by Kollen's count, attended an average seven thousand sermons in a lifetime, that meant they heard fifteen thousand hours of preaching from their pastor. (And of course that was pretty much *all* they heard, in an era with no theater, no library, no radio, no internet.) "Loyalists did not overestimate the power of anti-imperial rhetoric delivered from the pulpit."

For the Congregational clergy of this era (as, eventually, for Martin Luther King), the keystone story from the Bible was Exodus—the colonies were the British Israel, and the flight from Egypt was like the Pilgrim voyage to the New World. As opposition to London mounted, Clarke—the best-educated man in town—was Lexington's voice, drafting the town's declarations on the Stamp Act or the tea tax. And it wasn't just words—when colonists began to boycott British items, the town's "daughters of liberty" would gather at the church with their spinning wheels—sometimes forty-five women in all—to produce homespun fabric, a tactic Gandhi would adopt 150 years later. (John Parker, the town's wheelwright as well as its militia captain, reported a spike in spinning wheel sales, and his troops soon had homespun uniforms.) In any event, it was Clarke who kept Lexington in a patriotic fervor; it was at Clarke's parsonage that Sam Adams and John Hancock were rousted by Paul Revere on the morning of April 19; it was Clarke who buried the eight men who fell on the Green, and who provided the first published eyewitness testimony that they had been shot while dispersing; it was Clarke who composed the text for the obelisk that marks their grave.

This was not atypical. We tend to think of religion as a conservative force, but often in American history, clergy would play a major role in spurring history forward. To give a Lexington example, consider the grandson of Captain Parker—Theodore Parker was born in 1810, thirty-five years after the battle, and became a pastor at the age of twenty-seven. He fell under the influence of the transcendentalists next door in Concord—Emerson, Bronson Alcott (father of Louisa May), Thoreau—and became a pillar of Unitarianism, the breakaway sect from Congregationalism that preached a more liberal interpretation of Scripture. Parker's Boston congregation grew to two thousand souls that met at the city's music hall (at 3 percent of the city's population, it was an early megachurch), and included William Lloyd Garrison, foremost abolitionist of the era. Parker himself was a leading antislavery man—he harbored fugitive slaves in his home and was an outspoken supporter of John Brown. He echoes down through U.S. history—in an 1853 speech, for instance, he declared his support for "a democracy—of all the people, by all the people, for all the people," a phrase that Lincoln spruced up a little for the Gettysburg Address. And, predicting the victory of abolitionism, he said, "I do not pretend to understand the moral universe, the arc is a long one, my eye reaches but little ways. I cannot calculate the curve and complete the figure by the experience of sight; I can divine it by conscience. But from what I see I am sure it *bends towards justice*." Compacted a little, it became a staple in Dr. King's talks, from Montgomery to Selma. President Obama loved the phrase so much he had it woven into a rug for the Oval Office.

Of course, it's just as easy to make the opposite argument from history: that Christianity is a baleful force, baptizing oppression and sanctifying the unspeakable. Remember Bishop Hancock, beloved pastor whose "personality, scholarship, and wisdom led to esteem" great enough that he served as the senior minister for the entire region, overseeing the ordination of scores of other pastors? In 1728, when he was fifty-seven and his sons had left home, making it more difficult for him to manage his farm, his congregation gave him a present: 85 pounds to purchase a slave. "The bill of sale in Hancock's handwriting refers to a 'certain Negro boy called Jack,' and later 'Negro Jack,'" Richard Kollen reports. "In this case Jack was likely a teenager, as Hancock could not afford to purchase a young slave whose productivity projected far into the future." Hancock apparently changed Jack's name to Cato—there was a well-documented fashion for giving classical names to slaves, and many were named Pompey or Brutus. "Slaves were signs of status in New England society. . . . Many country ministers purchased slaves in order to maintain a farm and remain free to write sermons and make pastoral visits."

I've been a part of three different denominations in my life— basically, whatever flavor of mainline Protestantism happened to hold sway in the places where I lived—and each of them comes with a history. As an infant in Southern California, I was baptized a Presbyterian; Presbyterianism is generally traced to the Reverend Francis Makemie, who organized the first American presbytery, or body of elders, in America in 1706. He was a slaveholder—when he died in 1708 his will distributed thirty-three enslaved persons among his heirs. Then, in Lexington, I was confirmed into the United Church of Christ, the direct theological descendant of those Puritans, back through Reverend Clarke and Bishop Hancock. The UCC lists among its key "theological grandparents" Jonathan Edwards, often regarded as among America's greatest theologians, a stern figure remembered best for his famous sermon "Sinners in the Hands of an Angry God." Edwards purchased several human beings—he traveled to Newport, Rhode Island, to buy the first, a fourteen-year-old girl named Venus, who had been kidnapped in Africa. Edwards, a frugal man, used the back of the bill of sale to write a sermon; in his will he described his slaves as "stock." As an adult I became a Methodist, again because that's what there was in the small and isolated rural town where I made my life. Methodism's British founder, John Wesley, was an opponent of slavery, and a brave one—he preached an antislavery sermon in Bristol, England's main slave-trading port, and indeed it caused a riot: "the terror and confusion were inexpressible; the people rushed upon each other with the utmost violence." But Methodism's first important American leader was a man named George Whitefield, who helped spark that first Great Awakening. Whitefield campaigned to allow slavery in Georgia, in order to maintain the plantation that supported an orphanage he had founded. He left fifty slaves in his will.

So: poisoned at the source. Or: inextricably bound with American history, listing and lurching with the turns of that story, sometimes helping progress and sometimes holding it back. The great Protestant denominations split over the Civil War, into Northern and Southern churches, some of which managed to reunite in the twentieth century and some of which did not. (The Southern Baptist Convention, now America's biggest Protestant denomination, formed in opposition to abolition.) The point, perhaps, is that there's no significant gap between American history and religion up until about 1970, the hinge year of this book in so many ways. Americans were so overwhelmingly religious that it makes little sense to think of almost any development—good, bad, violent, peaceful, regressive, progressive—as separate from

Christianity. For every settlement house spawned by the social
Gospel, a Klan chapter; for every Father Coughlin, a Dr. King.
Lexington was entirely typical in this regard—as it prospered
and grew in the years after World War II, organized religion was
a central part of life, entirely comfortable with the most mainstream currents of life, precisely because it was the mainstream.

In 1947, Hancock Church—my church, the building closest
to the site of the battle, named for Bishop Hancock, both beloved
and a slave owner—hosted the Trapp Family Singers for a concert. A few years after that, it began construction on a two-story
addition to house the ever-growing Sunday school. A few years
after that, in 1958, with two thousand members swelling the pews
past any kind of accommodation, it hived off a new church, Pilgrim Congregational. As that offshoot built its own sanctuary, it
met for worship in what was then the chapel of the Episcopal
Church, which was itself growing so fast it too was building a big
new edifice of its own. And it wasn't just Protestants. In 1955 the
town's first synagogue, Temple Emunah, was established; within
four years, more liberal members left to form a Reform congregation, Temple Isaiah; both prospered and grew. That's the same
year that the First Baptist Church broke ground for a new chapel
and educational wing. The various denominations were less com-
petitive than cooperative—it was an age of ecumenicism, and in
1962, Monsignor Casey, pastor of Saint Brigid's Catholic Church,
received not only the Lexington Brotherhood Award, but also a
citation from the National Conference of Christians and Jews for
"promoting the cause of good will and understanding."

Precisely the same thing was happening across the country. The
year 1946 was the high-water mark for marriages in the United

States, so soon lots of people were seeking out Sunday schools for their kids. Church administrators did their best to encourage the trend—signs announcing that "The Episcopal Church Welcomes You" became "regular fixtures in the expanding suburbs," one denominational history records, as planners watched real estate trends and planted churches wherever subdivisions sprouted. In 1958, according to religious historian Mark Silk, "*52 out of every 100 Americans were affiliated with a mainline Protestant denomination*"—that is, they were a Congregationalist, a Lutheran, a northern Baptist, a Methodist, an Episcopalian. In that year, President Dwight Eisenhower—who had been baptized into the mainline Presbyterian church ten days after taking office, and who had signed into law a revision to the Pledge of Allegiance adding the words "under God"—laid the cornerstone for the Interchurch Center in New York, catty-corner from John D. Rockefeller's Riverside Church. The Interchurch Center—known alternately as the God Box or the Protestant Kremlin—was headquarters for several of those denominations and also for the National Council of Churches. It would be, Eisenhower said, "the national home of the churches." The United States, he said, was politically free because it was religiously free, in contrast to its Cold War opponents. "Without this firm foundation, national morality could not be maintained."

Anything this broad, of course, was necessarily bland. These churches worshipped the Christ of Warner Sallman's 1940 painting, with "smooth white skin, long flowing brown hair, a full beard, and blue eyes"—a portrait printed 500 million times. (As Jemar Tisby points out in his remarkable history *The Color of Compromise*, "one Lutheran from Chicago distributed wallet-sized pictures of Sallman's Christ so that 'card-carrying Christians' could oppose 'card-carrying Communists.'") Leading evangelicals were moderate too: Reverend Billy Graham invited Reverend Martin Luther King to give the opening prayer at one of his rallies in 1957 (and then advised him privately to "put on the brakes" with the activism).

But this Christianity, if moderate to a fault, also had intellectual heft. The theologian Paul Tillich was on the cover of *Time* in 1959: the journalist explains that the Harvard theologian was from Germany, "which produces philosophers and theologians as Australia produces tennis players," and then goes on gamely and hopelessly to try and explain Tillich's "all-important distinction between religious 'heteronomy,' which is imposed upon the individual, and religious 'autonomy,' in which the individual continually seeks and hopes to find." Reinhold Niebuhr was on the cover of *Time* too, and this time his chronicler (of all people, Whittaker Chambers, in his last big piece of journalism before starting on his crusade against supposed Communist spies in the U.S. government) was at pains to make clear that, though a liberal, Niebuhr is "the leading liberal opponent of pacifism. . . . He is also an opponent of Marxism." He's not, however, an opponent of "the pursuit of happiness which modern civilization, more than any other, has legitimatized. But he implies that the pursuit of happiness loses measure, just as optimism loses reality, if neither is aware of what Wordsworth called 'the still sad music of humanity.'" These Christian theologians were serious, and they were revered; it's been a while since *Time* put a theologian on the cover.

I was born into this world, literally. My parents carried me to church in the early 1960s in Pasadena, California, where they themselves revered a minister named Ganse Little, a fourth-generation preacher who was soon installed as moderator of the Presbyterian Church, then 3.3 million members strong. In Pasadena, he had taken over the pulpit from Eugene Carson Blake, who went on to become general secretary of the World Council of Churches. Blake graced the cover of *Time* as well, four months after my birth, when he was described as "a square-jawed, hazel-eyed man of action, whose three euphonious names have become synonymous in church circles with efficient organization, knowing diplomacy, and zeal for unity." Indeed, the magazine described his recent appeal to Methodists, Presbyterians, Congregationalists, and Episcopalians that they unite to form one giant Protestant church. As *Time* pointed out, in a newly mobile suburban nation, "Americans on the move to new communities today tend to take their faiths with them, but they switch them easily under a variety of influences. They tend more and more to pick their churches because they are within walking distance, or because their friends go there, or because they like the preacher."

If all of this makes the church sound like a comfortable civic institution—the Rotary Club at prayer—there's clearly plenty of truth to that. People joined to conform, and in that conformity found community. As King pointed out in his talk in Lexington in 1963, eleven o'clock on Sunday morning was the most segregated hour in America. "There is more integration in a side street tavern than a front street church," he said, and of course that segregation muffled and dampened the response to injustice. His "Letter from Birmingham Jail," with its famous words about white moderates, was addressed to a group of mostly Protestant clergy who had urged him to pursue civil rights through litigation, not demonstration. As he said in Lexington, many churches have "a high blood pressure of creeds, and an anemia of deeds."

And yet it wasn't altogether like that. In Lexington, it was clergy who had traveled south to join in the march at Selma, and who assembled a vast memorial service on the Green for the minister who was killed there. It was an alliance of interfaith groups that pushed for affordable housing, even threatening to sue the town. It was the ministers who stood up for, and with, the Vietnam Veterans Against the War when they marched on the Green. I hadn't completely understood how committed they were until I was reading the oral histories of that Battle Green fight. Robert Cataldo, you'll remember, was the chair of the Board of Selectmen and the one who ultimately made the decision to call in the police who arrested my father. His account of the action is fairly restrained ("in my opinion it's healthy to have a difference of opinion and a cross-section of people") until the questioner asks him about the role of the churches.

"The clergy put the town in that position," he insists, and you can almost hear him begin to splutter through the pages of the transcript. "The clergy supported the veterans every inch of the way, to do what they did. The clergy got involved in it. In my opinion, it's not their role. The clergy has a responsibility to the townspeople. I think that, basically, they should not have been involved in this issue."

INTERVIEWER: What clergy were they?

ROBERT CATALDO: Every one of them.

INTERVIEWER: Every one of them?

ROBERT CATALDO: Missing none.

INTERVIEWER: What church did you belong to at the time?

ROBERT CATALDO: Sacred Heart.

INTERVIEWER: Who was the pastor there at the time?

ROBERT CATALDO: Father McKay. And Father Kelty had been in Saint Brigid's. And I was livid with them.

INTERVIEWER: And did they use the pulpit at times—at all— in terms of sermons to talk about the war?

ROBERT CATALDO: I was so mad at them I wouldn't go to church.

INTERVIEWER: So they were very, very active.

ROBERT CATALDO: Very active, very active, every one of them.

So what was it like to be a kid in one of those churches that were, then, so much a part of American life, and now—just fifty years later—so peripheral? I was ten when we joined Hancock Church, so my early memories are scattered, fragmentary. The minister was a man named Henry Clark, who had been called to the pulpit in 1954; I remember a big-shouldered man, a deep voice, a kind eye, seen on Sunday in robes—God, essentially. But my world was the world of the Sunday school: my first teacher, an older woman named Jackie Childs, told me later that her only real goal was to make her charges simply like coming to church, and she succeeded. For reasons not entirely clear to me now, my first task was to build an Egyptian pyramid out of sugar cubes and vanilla frosting, a task I enjoyed considerably more than did the Jews who had labored for Pharaoh.

We must have had the run of the place—I know this because
I can remember where the boiler room was, and what it was
like to be in the balcony above the sanctuary listening to the
organist rehearse; I watched the ushers count the money from
the offering plates, and helped take the flowers off the altar for
distribution to the "shut-ins." By seventh grade, in the junior
division of the youth group, we'd be shuttled off to the denomination's conference center on Cape Cod for weekends two or
three times a year—"retreats" that were the first times I spent
nights away from my family. They were necessarily hormonal
and rambunctious, but also centering: that's where "Kumbaya"
entered my life.

By high school those trips became more serious—in fact, the
highlight of the year was a weeklong "service" trip over spring
break to someplace far away and very different. I remember the
first one the best. We got on a rented bus and drove straight
through the day and night till we reached a rural corner of North
Carolina, where we worked five days scraping and painting at
some kind of conference center that must have belonged to the
Black church—at least, everyone we saw was Black. At night the
darkness fell in a way I'd never known, and we'd walk through
it down dirt roads—there was a railroad track, and once every
night the train would crash open the night with light and noise,
and then everything would subside back into a deeper silence.
There were more stars than I'd ever seen. One night there was
a party, in the dark—it was with the Black kids from the surrounding area, who seemed as surprised as we were. (The local
town, after *Brown v. Board of Education*, had built a segregated
"Christian academy," so they lived a life not much more diverse

than ours.) Someone had a radio; flashlights provided enough illumination for a *Soul Train*–style dance line; happily some of the senior girls from our group possessed sufficient rhythm that we weren't entirely embarrassed. The next day we set out Easter eggs in the lawn for the small kids to hunt. We ate grits.

Back home, every Friday a few of us from the youth group would gather after school at the church and take someone's car out to the edge of town, where we visited what was called the Fernald State School for the Retarded (an improvement on its original name, "the Experimental School for Teaching and Training Idiotic Children"). It served then as a warehouse for people with nowhere else to go (again, an improvement—the Fernald for whom it was named had been a superintendent focused on eugenics and sterilization: in the '40s and '50s residents were dosed with radioactive calcium to trace its absorption in the blood). I don't really know why the authorities there, or back at church, thought it was wise to send a small squad of unsupervised fifteen-year-olds into the middle of this, but it was a different time. Anyway, we went each week to a "dayroom" that housed perhaps four hundred women, who sat there all afternoon doing not much. When we walked through the door, a murmur would crescendo almost into a roar, and people would descend on us— hugs, babble. It was incredibly hot, and it smelled as you would expect, and I went back week after week, year after year. There was a woman, Marjorie, who became a friend—she was more cognitively able than anyone around her, and one day I found her weeping. She'd watched a TV show the night before about Down syndrome, and figured out who she was, and where she was.

My senior year the spring trip went to a town called Frogmore in South Carolina. Again we were painting and scraping, this time at a complex called Penn Center, founded by missionaries in 1862 as the first school for African Americans in the South. As the Civil War ended, it provided critical services for the area's Gullah slaves after plantation owners fled the area. (These were the precise people who gave us "Kumbaya.") A decade before our visit, and months before his death, this is the place where Martin Luther King had come with his staff to plan the Poor People's Campaign. So full circle in lots of ways.

I am well aware now that all of these actions had more to do with charity than justice—that they would probably now fall under the general rubric of "white savior complex." And I'm aware that those are sound cautions. When we were at Frogmore, our college acceptance letters were arriving back home; when we got off the bus we went home to envelopes that held the tickets to an easy kind of future. Still, for some of us, *contact* with a larger and harder reality was an enormous gift. And it was important to have contact in a setting—the church—that helped me understand it was my job to do something about it. I have no doubt that those years helped set the course of my life.

In any event, I tell the story because that world no longer really exists. Hancock Church continues, and robustly—if its membership is reduced, it still has superb preaching and music and Sunday school. It continues to do good works with relish; each year for the last dozen its youth group has headed down over spring break to a small town in Appalachian Kentucky to build and refurbish. But the world in which it lives is very different.

I said before that in 1958, when Dwight Eisenhower laid

the cornerstone of that Interchurch Center in New York and
declared it the "national home of the churches," fifty-two out of
every one hundred Americans belonged to one of the mainline
Protestant denominations it represented. By 2016 that number
had dropped to thirteen. That is, the percentage of the population that inhabited this world had been reduced by three-
quarters. It's true that the population of the country has almost
doubled, but that hasn't been enough to stop the decline in total
numbers, which had started to affect all these denominations by
1970 and basically never stopped. Those who remain are old: 4.5
percent of the population beneath the age of thirty-five belongs
to a mainline church, as opposed to 20.6 percent of the population over sixty-five. The median age of the American population is forty-six years old; all the mainline denominations have
a median age of fifty-seven or higher. Basically, these traditions
have begun to die out.

That happens to institutions of all kinds, of course—there
were a thousand Howard Johnson's restaurants in America in
midcentury too; under the orange roof was "arguably the most
popular place to eat in the United States," according to the *Wall
Street Journal*. Now there's a single HoJo's left, so almost certainly you will never again know the pleasures of their fried
clam strips or root beer floats. As one nostalgic customer told
the *Journal* reporter, "They were happy places. Wherever in the
country you and your parents might be driving, they were waiting for you. When you were a child and you went inside, you
felt safe and calm, and even though you'd never been in that
particular one before, you somehow felt like you were home."
Which is a pretty good description of the suburban church in

those days. But Howard Johnson's gave way not to fasting, but to McDonald's and Burger King and Pizza Hut; people eat out far more than they ever did. That's not precisely what happened with Christianity. As we'll see, over the first part of the last fifty years, evangelicals fared better than mainline Protestants, but now that's passed too—now those churches may even be dwindling faster. It's really Christianity—and religious belonging in general—that's on the decline.

When I was born in 1960, and even when I moved to Lexington in 1970, 97 percent of the American population told survey researchers they believed in God; 95 percent were sure of his existence (and though it hadn't yet occurred to anyone to ask, most of them would certainly have said "his"). By 2021, for the first time in eighty years of measuring, the percentage of Americans who belonged to a church or synagogue or mosque had dropped below half, according to Gallup—just 47 percent of Americans claimed membership in some religious institution. Barely a third of millennials were members. And of the people who do still belong, that belonging seems to mean less: fewer than a quarter of Americans attend services at churches or synagogues every week. What's rising are the "nones," people who claim no religious faith; some are atheists or agnostics, and some are "spiritual," but they don't go to church—and if they were a denomination, they'd outnumber the mainline Protestants. They'd outnumber Catholics. They'd outnumber evangelicals. Especially among young people.

At least in certain subcultures, we've reached the point where religious involvement is a curiosity, even a source of some shame.

I'm on the faculty of a truly wonderful college that attracts incredibly bright young people from all fifty states and many foreign countries for four years in rural Vermont. Compared to me at the age of eighteen, their accomplishments are incredible: they *arrive* knowing Arabic or Chinese. But they are, by and large, entirely divorced from the religious culture that would, a generation or two before, have been ubiquitous. A few years ago I was teaching a course on nonviolent social movements, and we were reading about Dr. King, who had relied (like the colonial patriots and the abolitionists) on the story of Exodus with its theme of collective liberation. But it soon became clear that of the thirty students in the room, almost none had any idea about Moses and the wilderness. Two or three of the kids, working together, could piece together a reasonable account of the crucifixion (the most adept was a Korean, from the country where mainline Protestantism may be strongest). Not only is the resurrection the foundational story of Western civilization; it's hard to completely comprehend nonviolent action, which derives its power from unearned suffering, without any reference to the cross. So I decided to teach a course on "Stories from the Bible," and it was a delight: we barely made it out of Genesis before the semester was over because we were having so much fun. But part of the delight was that no one, even though they'd chosen to take the course, knew much of anything at all about the subject—it was like teaching horticulture to Martians. We worked our way through Cain murdering Abel and drunk and naked Noah and the hubris of Babel, through Jacob cheating Esau, and Joseph's brothers tossing him in a hole—after all of that, one of the students stayed after class to talk. "I'm really enjoying this," she said. "But I'm confused. I always thought the Bible was about good people." Ah well.

I DON'T TELL these stories or recite these statistics with a sense of mourning; even if there was a Howard Johnson's still around the corner, the chances I'd bother to go eat there are small. In a very real sense this shift makes for a healthier country: 65 percent of those "nones" voted for Joe Biden in 2020, which is as close to a referendum on good moral sense as we'll ever get. But a change this large—and again, it dwarfs every other demographic shift in our country in my lifetime—doesn't happen without both reflecting and causing other shifts. It's worth trying to understand.

Part of it is simple math. Mainline Protestants were at the top of the economic heap, and people at the top of the economic heap have lower birth rates: towns like Lexington were closing schools in the '80s and '90s as fast as they'd built them in the '50s and '60s. And immigrants were no longer coming from places where Lutheranism or Presbyterianism was standard.

But that wasn't all. As with most establishments, this one was . . . dull, almost as a matter of principle. Methodists were indeed methodical, officially describing their faith as relying on the "Wesleyan quadrilateral" of the Bible, tradition, reason, and experience. Episcopalians took pride in their commitment to the *via media*, the middle way. The historian and essayist Diana Butler Bass, who has devoted her life to understanding this period in American Christianity, wrote once:

many people are just bored. . . . Many of my friends, faithful
churchgoers for decades, are dropping out because religion
is dull, the purview of folks who never want to change or
always want to fight about somebody else's sex life. . . . On
Sundays, other things are more interesting—the *New York
Times*, sports, shopping, Facebook, family time, working in
the garden, biking, hiking, sipping lattes at the local coffee
shop, meeting up at the dog park, getting the kids to the soccer game.

In Jonas Clarke's day as a preacher in the 1770s, he was the
only person in Lexington with a library; by the time I arrived
and Henry Clark was in the pulpit, his congregation included a
score of college professors. It was the same everywhere: church
was not required for intellectual stimulation, and in the same
way that people grew less tolerant of bad coffee, they had less
interest in mediocre preaching.

Since the mainline was, by definition, in the middle, it had the
hardest time of all the religious groupings. Its theology and worship styles were, to put it politely, firmly rooted in the past. Baby
boomers, Bass notes, began to "desert their childhood churches,"
finding them "tedious" and "out of touch." But when the churches
"tried to be more relevant and attempted to change, many older
members protested by withdrawing financial support or by leaving themselves." (I belonged to a rural Methodist church that
nearly foundered on the pastor's desire to change the name in an
effort to attract new congregants—people who had not been to
a service in decades showed up for the meeting to defend "the
way it's always been.") The old mainline, she writes, "could not

please anyone. Congregations moved, combined, or closed in an effort to save money and resources. As the membership decline progressed, internal conflict increased, and bitter denominational battles ensued. Observers nicknamed them the 'old-line' or the 'side-lined' churches."

It's true that leaders of these traditions had often behaved honorably in the battles of the 1960s. When Dr. King asked ministers to join civil rights marchers in Selma in March of 1965, they poured in by the hundreds from around the country; one from Boston, a Presbyterian turned Unitarian named James Reeb, was beaten to death. If you go to the chapel of the Episcopal Divinity School in Cambridge, there's a stained-glass window commemorating Jonathan Daniels, gunned down later that summer in Alabama shielding a seventeen-year-old Black girl from a shotgun blast. (King called it "one of the most heroic Christian deeds of which I have heard in my entire ministry.") The same theme played out in many places: that's why Robert Cataldo, the selectman, was so vehement in his attack on "the churches" that conspired to oppose the war. But again, it all went only so far. In Lexington the interfaith alliance wasn't strong enough to win the referendum on affordable housing and truly integrate the town. And in many other places, as Robert Jones makes clear in *White Too Long*, his compelling history of the period, the churches were complicit in ongoing segregation, "protecting and improving white Christians' lives within an unjust social status quo, which is to say a context of extreme racial inequality and injustice." Jemar Tisby cites a study from Chicago documenting the way that the Reformed churches in neighborhood after neighborhood assisted the blockbusters by relocating to the white suburbs as their parishioners began to desert the inner city. "Rather than stay and adapt to a new community reality or assist in integrating the neighborhood, many white churches chose to depart."

Important symbolic and practical gestures were made: in 1989, say, the Episcopalians installed a female bishop, Barbara Harris, for the first time. In June of 2003 the same church elected its first gay bishop, Gene Robinson. These were obvious steps, reflecting the reality of a changing secular world. I'd met Robinson at a church retreat where I was speaking about climate change a few months before his ascension, and it is hard to imagine a milder character; the fact that he was soon having to wear a bulletproof vest was astonishing. But in fact every such step was fought bitterly, by those who couldn't bring themselves to come to terms with change. Each of the mainline denominations spawned an internal conservative opposition movement, usually well funded by businessmen of the kind who were building other right-wing political movements. They proved savvy at exploiting the mainline traditions of tolerance and civility—in most cases liberal Christians combined their inclusive politics with a polite deference that kept them from making a final breach with their opponents, who often wore them down over time. (My Methodists are still, in 2022, in the process of shaking themselves apart over the question of treating gay people as full human beings; it seems likely the denomination will split on the same regional lines as it did before the Civil War, but not before losing most of its younger members.) And so the world moved on.

· · · · ·

THE DECLINE OF the once dominant mainline church was a third of the story; the rise of the nones another third; and the final part, of course, was the even more explosive ascension of an evangelical and usually conservative Christianity. We need to pay that story some due, but I'm not going to tell it at any great length—it's been told many times, and ably.

And before I even begin telling it, I have another tale to relate, this one firsthand. In the early 1980s, as a young reporter for my college paper, I headed south over spring break to write about a man named Jim Bakker, one of the early exemplars of the new megachurch TV-pastor evangelism, who was sometimes held out as the next Billy Graham. Bakker—and his wife, Tammy Faye—headquartered their PTL (Praise the Lord) Club just across the state line from Charlotte in Fort Mill, South Carolina, where they built a vast destination resort called Heritage USA; by the mid-1980s it was the third-biggest tourist attraction in America, trailing only the Disney theme parks in Anaheim and Orlando. And I went there to make fun of it, which wasn't hard. An aide met me at the shining ziggurat that served as the headquarters; in the basement he showed me a vast room filled with women who were slitting open envelopes and shaking out checks (and prayer requests); a million dollars a week or more was flooding in. I sat in the control room as the daily broadcast taped: a producer would tell Tammy Faye through her earpiece that it was time to cry, and within seconds tears would be cutting rivulets through her thick makeup. Wandering the vast spread—ten times the size of Disneyland—was a hallucinatory experience: there was a fiberglass "Kings Castle," slated to become the largest Wendy's restaurant in the world, and a life-size version of the Upper Room where the Last Supper had been conducted, and Billy Graham's actual boyhood home, and a Heavenly Fudge Factory, and the planet's biggest wave pool. My mockery of this temple of grift was entirely justified—within a few years it emerged that Bakker had been selling far more time-share condos on the site than he'd actually built, and that he was diverting some of the proceeds to pay hush money to a secretary, Jessica Hahn, who accused him of raping her in a Florida hotel room. It was the prototypical evangelical story, full of internecine warfare. (Bakker was dimed out by competing televangelist Jimmy Swaggart, who called him "a cancer in the body of Christ," and who was himself promptly caught visiting prostitutes in New Orleans; the PTL empire was taken over by Jerry Falwell, whose namesake son would eventually end up being sued by Liberty University after he left its presidency amid charges that he'd given huge sums to a pool boy for the pleasure of watching him have sex with Falwell's wife.) Parts of the PTL property have since been owned by Morris Cerullo, later indicted for tax evasion in California, where he built his own vast Christian amusement park complete with catacomb.

And yet. On my last night at the PTL Club, out of money and preparing to drive all the way back to Boston with nothing but my father's Texaco charge card to get me there, I went to the nightly church service in the Jerusalem Amphitheater. (Bakker never did get around to finishing his plans for a "full-size replica of Jerusalem in the time of Jesus," but he did construct this open-air pavilion.) The service was fairly tawdry—there was a hype man telling jokes to get the audience going before the main act came on, and while I can't remember a word of the sermon, I can say with confidence that it was mawkish. As it ended, though, an

older man in the pew in front of me turned around and said quietly, "God told me to give you this," and he handed me a twenty-
dollar bill. Which I took. I would have gotten home without it,
but it meant I got home with a couple of sandwiches in my belly.
More, I got home with a good reminder not to sneer so much.

Even so, it was hard for me to take the rise of evangelicalism entirely seriously, for so much of it seemed so unprincipled,
even grotesque. And yet, from small beginnings (the National
Association of Evangelicals was founded in 1942, representing
about two million members, at a time when the mainline Protestants spoke for sixty or seventy million Americans), it grew
into a juggernaut: think Pat Robertson, VeggieTales, Rick Warren, Amy Grant, Promise Keepers. Reacting to the "permissive-
ness" of the 1960s, reacting to the infidels of 9/11, reacting to
the threat of gay marriage, they were always reaching backward
for a vision of something from before (Heritage USA!). Right-
wing Christianity was, of course, one of the forces that powered
Ronald Reagan's transformational rise to the presidency (over
Jimmy Carter, an honest-to-God devout Baptist), and it now
anchors the Trump movement: Trump took more than 80 percent of white evangelical voters in both 2016 and 2020, despite
(or because of) the fact that he was a philandering philistine.
Its engrained racism goes almost without saying: historians are
clear that the original trigger for right-wing Christian activism
wasn't abortion (which the Southern Baptist Convention con-
doned in the 1970s) but the loss of tax exemptions for the white
"Christian academies" that sprang up in the wake of *Brown v.
Board of Education*. As Robert Jones points out in *White Too
Long*, the best way to predict how often a white evangelical will

go to church is to know his score on an index of racial feelings (the more racist, the more hours in the pews).

Trumpism was the logical endpoint of all of this: on election night in 2016, Franklin Graham (the hard-right son of Billy) texted Mike Pence to say, "Look at what God did tonight." Pence texted back: "Isn't it awesome?" Nothing that happened in the next few years shook the faith: the massive turnout of white evangelicals was the reason Trump wasn't more badly beaten in 2020 (though only 15 percent of the population, evangelicals represented about a quarter of the electorate), and in any event they didn't believe he had been bested. Eric Metaxas (who had published the children's books *Donald Drains the Swamp* and *Donald Builds the Wall*) had Trump on his radio show after the election to say, of the battle to overturn the election, "Jesus is with us in this fight for liberty. I'd be happy to die in this fight." When the Capitol was invaded, rioters carried signs saying, "Jesus 2020." Outside on the Mall they chanted, "Christ is King."

You know all this, which is one reason I won't belabor it. And evangelicalism has been, in certain ways, less successful than it seems. For all the ability to elect presidents, it hasn't been able to roll back the ideas that first gained hold in the 1960s and have continued to spread. Mainline Protestantism's cultural power has, in some sense, held; the intolerance and hatred of the religious right eventually began to erode its own base. As early as 2007, a survey by the Barna Group found that only 3 percent of non-Christians below the age of thirty had favorable opinions of evangelicalism. They described it as "judgmental" (87 percent), "hypocritical" (81 percent), and "old-fashioned" (75 percent). The most common perception among young non-Christians—and again, this was as early as 2007—was that it was "anti-homosexual." Ninety-one percent of young people believed that—but even more interestingly, 80 percent of young evangelicals believed it. Only 16 percent of young adults outside the faith said that Christianity "consistently shows love for other people." Considering the theoretical tenets of the faith ("You shall love your neighbor as yourself"), this is a failure of fairly epic proportions. It's no wonder that reactionary Christians, even when they win elections, feel embattled.

But the other reason I won't belabor the rise of evangelicalism is that I don't think, in the end, it's the most important underlying change. I think something else even more powerful has been going on, something related to the suburbs and prosperity, something that undergirds these remarkable shifts in religious understanding. And that's the replacement of a sense of community with a sense of hyper-individualism.

HANCOCK CHURCH, WHERE I went, was the biggest and most important Protestant church in town in those days, its history stretching back to those colonial pastors, exemplifying the power of that mainline consensus. As one member from that era recalled recently for a church history, you "couldn't get elected to town office in Lexington without being a member of the Hancock Men's Club."

But a contender was growing that would surpass it.

Five families began meeting for worship in a basement beginning in 1948; by 1959 they'd raised $100,000 to construct Grace

Chapel—they called it a chapel "because the founders envisioned a small church, no more than a hundred families." But it continued to grow, drawing families from across a wide swath of suburbia. When I was a cub reporter for the local paper in my high school summers, the editor sent me off to look into the phenomenon. I remember meeting with several members of the ministerial team. Unlike my minister, they in no way resembled God; instead they had the polo shirts and the upbeat attitude of softball coaches at an on-the-rise junior college. And what they talked about was *growth*: they were about to open a new sanctuary that would hold fourteen hundred people. It would be the largest auditorium in town, the twelfth largest in metropolitan Boston. And they would have no problem, they insisted, filling it every Sunday. Twice every Sunday. "We anticipate an almost instant 25 percent growth," one of them said. "The only thing holding back our growth is lack of space." Indeed, "we are the fastest growing church in New England."

Curious, I went to a few services, and I was instantly struck by how different it was from church as I knew it—and how much it was like everything else. In place of a preacher behind a pulpit, there were worship leaders holding microphones—the long kind, on a stalk, that were common then on talk shows. Indeed, the ministers talked back and forth, and people emerged from the wings to sing: it was a TV show. Having watched lots of TV, I felt very much at home: it was Mike Douglas or Merv Griffin, but about religion. And in place of the gravitas that settled over the Hancock sanctuary as the service began, there was a consistently cheerful air, a joy that felt slightly forced but alluring. This was the mall; again, having spent a fair amount of time in the food court, I felt at home.

I also, of course, thought it was tacky—I'd already spent too many years in the more austere confines of old New England Congregationalism not to disdain the glitz. But I also knew that television, and shopping malls, were . . . successful. At some level I knew I was seeing the future. So it didn't surprise me over the next decades as this became one of—probably *the*—archetypal experiences of worship in America. The megachurch—Willow Creek, or Saddleback, or all the other variations that spread across the country—could be analyzed in political terms: they certainly tilted right, and many became important players in the various political pathologies from the Moral Majority to the Trump campaign. But that was not, I think, the crucial axis. Instead of placing them on a spectrum from liberal to conservative, place them on a spectrum from citizen to consumer, or of community to individual.

The next big chunk of this book—the part about the station wagon—will have a lot to say about the rise of hyper-individualism: it turns out to be the key, I think, to our political evolution (and to the fact that the Arctic ice cap is mostly melted). But it's notable that we can see the same phenomenon playing out in our religious life.

There'd always been a tension in Protestantism, of course, between the individual and the community. The whole separation from Catholicism—the very thing that Luther was *protest*ing about—had to do with the "priesthood of all believers," the idea that each individual has direct access to God without any real need for priests or popes. Forget the spiritual hierarchy stretching up to Rome: you could reach out to God on your own; you could read the Bible by yourself. You—your soul—was the center of the drama. But this had been coupled with the concrete reality of the community of believers: all those pilgrims shipping out together, all those colonial farmers crowding each Sunday into the meetinghouse. All those Eisenhower-era parents signing their kids up for Sunday school and coming to church because it was an accepted part of life.

The "cure" for that conformity was an explosion of individualism. For some people that looked like hippiedom (we would, in the early 1970s, take the bus into Harvard Square and wander around awestruck), and for some people (sometimes the same people) it took the form of this highly individual relationship with "my Lord and personal savior Jesus Christ." All of it curdled into consumerism, to the point where it's almost unrecognizable as connected to Tillich or Niebuhr or to the kind of church I grew up with.

The remarkable literary critic James Woods, writing in the *New Yorker*, describes his own transition as a child from the "stolid Anglican church" the family had attended to "one that was undergoing what was known as a charismatic renewal," focused on precisely this kind of personal and almost mercenary relationship with God. "When my mother told the pastor that I had done well on a recent school exam, he gave me a hug and offered a hearty 'Praise the Lord!'" rather in the manner of basketball stars that immediately and somewhat improbably credit Jesus with their victories. I'm grateful to Wood for introducing me to the work of T. M. Luhrmann, a Stanford anthropologist who spent hundreds of hours interviewing megachurch attendees about their spiritual lives.

Among her interviewees, Elaine prays for guidance about whether to take a roommate or move to a new apartment. Kate gets angry with God and "yells at him when things go wrong—when she organizes a trip for the church and the bus company is flaky or it rains." Stacy prays for a good haircut, and Hannah asks God about whom to date, and sometimes feels he is pranking her in little ways: "I'll trip and fall, and I'll be like, *Thanks, God.*" Rachel asks for help with how to dress: "Like, God, what should I wear? . . . I think God cares about really, really little things in my life."

This neediness goes both ways. I'm always struck, watching services at such churches, how much of the time is spent reassuring God that he's great. "We praise your name, O Lord" begins almost every prayer and interrupts every paragraph. The praise song repertoire that dominates worship at such churches always sounds slightly desperate to my ears—here's the much-loved "What a Beautiful Name":

> What a beautiful Name it is
> What a beautiful Name it is
> The Name of Jesus Christ my King
> What a beautiful Name it is
> Nothing compares to this
> What a beautiful Name it is
> The Name of Jesus

And of course this hyper-individualism extends to the many people who left church behind altogether—the people who tell pollsters in huge numbers that they are "spiritual but not religious." By the mid-1980s the sociologist Robert Bellah was already identifying this new strand in our life, introducing readers of his best-selling *Habits of the Heart* to "Sheila Larson, a young nurse who has received a good deal of therapy and describes her faith as 'Sheilaism.' This suggests the logical possibility of more than 235 million American religions, one for each of us. 'I believe in God,' Sheila says. 'I am not a religious fanatic. I can't remember the last time I went to church. My faith has carried me a long way. It's Sheilaism. Just my own little voice.' Sheila's faith has some tenets beyond belief in God, though not many. In defining what she calls 'my own Sheilaism,' she said: 'It's just try to love yourself and be gentle with yourself.'"

Its purest expression, though, was in those sprawling megachurches. And their sense of the world turned out to have huge political implications. In 2001, a pair of sociologists—Michael Emerson and Christian Smith—published a landmark book, *Divided by Faith*, which lays out what they call a "cultural tool kit" used by white evangelicals—the "ideas, habits, skills, and styles" that help them organize experience and evaluate reality. The key component is what they call "accountable individualism," the idea that "individuals exist independent of structures and institutions, have freewill, and are individually accountable for their own actions." Absent "from their accounts is the idea that poor relationships might be shaped by social structures, such as laws, the ways institutions operate, or forms of segregation." As a result, 62 percent of white evangelicals attribute poverty among Black Americans to a lack of motivation. Only 27 percent think the wealth gap between Black and white Americans comes from racial discrimination.

Or think about the way that evangelicals responded to the coronavirus pandemic. Christians first got noticed in the ancient world in part because the small sect was willing to act courageously in the face of plague—Dionysius, bishop of Alexandria in the third century, when two-thirds of the population died in one pestilence, reported, "most of our brother Christians showed unbounded love and loyalty, never sparing themselves and thinking only of one another." Martin Luther didn't flee Wittenberg when the bubonic plague struck in 1572—instead, the professor of theology stayed there to care for patients. In an open letter titled "Whether One May Flee from a Deadly Plague," he wrote that one should "act like a man who wants to help put out the burning city." And he was wise enough, in the sixteenth century, to understand social distancing: "I shall avoid places and persons where my presence is not needed in order not to become contaminated and thus perchance infect and pollute others, and so cause their death as a result of my negligence." By contrast, for too many evangelicals in twenty-first-century America, COVID was simply a moment to feel put upon, constrained. As *New Yorker* writer Michael Luo explained, "the lasting image of the Church in the pandemic may well be that of an unmasked choir at First Baptist Church, in Dallas, led by the pastor Robert Jeffress, a staunch Trump supporter, singing in front of Vice President Mike Pence at a 'Freedom Sunday' service as the county where the church is located reported a record high for COVID-19 cases." Among white evangelicals, the more you went to church, the more likely you were to refuse the vaccine—never mind that it was the most obvious, easy way to help others around you. That's gone; what's left in the evangelical world is a consumer, transactional relationship. As Robert Jones, in his study of white churches, put it, "Jesus is conceived of as a savior figure because he does what individual humans cannot: he reconciles human beings to God by sacrificing his life to atone for human sin. . . . In the personal Jesus paradigm, Jesus did not die for a cause or for humankind writ large but for each individual person."

IT'S NOT THAT right-wing evangelicalism is going to replace mainline Protestantism—the Southern Baptists are currently losing members more quickly than the United Methodists. It's that nothing is going to replace it. Catholicism has produced a genuinely popular pope in Francis, and the Biden administration has come with a nostalgic nod to the liberal era of Vatican II and the Kennedys—but church membership among Catholics has fallen even faster than among Protestants, in part no doubt because of the endless fallout from sex abuse scandals. Atheism is on a glide path up: the youngest cohort of Americans, Gen Z, is twice as likely to claim it as any of their predecessors. Immigration, especially from Asia, means that there are small increases in the "other" category: Hinduism and Buddhism will, like Judaism and Islam, be durable parts of American life. But there's not going to be a religious consensus like the one I grew up with. The conformity that may have ordered, and stifled, the suburbs of the 1960s has been overcome—you can argue about the costs and benefits, but not, I think, the fact of it. If you wanted to be dramatic, you could say that for the first time since Constantine, Americans who trace their ancestry to Europe are living in a non-Christian nation. A post-Christian nation.

Since Constantine's Council of Nicaea was in 325, and 325 was a long time ago, we don't have a great deal of experience in that kind of world. We can get some sense of what it feels like by looking across the Atlantic—Western Europe was a generation ahead of America in its secularization. But it will be different here, and it's too early to tell how it will play out. Diana Butler Bass has been the great Protestant chronicler of this shift: "The process of leaving religion, one that started three or four decades ago, seems to have reached a tipping point. We have most likely come to the end of the beginning of a great transformation of faith. What was is no longer," she wrote, and therefore for some Christians "discontent, doubt, disillusionment, and for some, despair are the themes of the day." Indeed, for some conservative Christians, decampment is the order of the day—they've embraced a "Benedict Option," heading for enclaves far from the secular bustle where they can build schools and raise families together and wait.

But for Christians who hope to see the world change—who hope to see a fairer planet, and one that might ward off the deepest threats to Creation—then there's something to be said for living in this post-Christian world. Yes, it's true that being part of that broad moderate consensus offered a certain kind of power to make things a little better: that was the world I've described, where all the pastors in Lexington could welcome Dr. King to give a talk, and could join him in Selma; the world where they could guard the veterans on Lexington Green.

INTERVIEWER: What clergy were they?

ROBERT CATALDO: Every one of them.

INTERVIEWER: Every one of them?

ROBERT CATALDO: Missing none.

So, honor to those people in that place and time. In the last "justice moment" in American history they played a very real part: the successes of Dr. King's civil rights movement depended on the shared religious vocabulary that made it impossible for people to simply ignore his appeal.

But let's be clear about the limits of that power: they couldn't persuade the people of Lexington, in the privacy of a voting booth, to back affordable housing. That power was limited by the very fact of its enormous reach: if everyone was in church, then, broadly speaking, the brute demographic power of that *everyone* was shaping theology at least as thoroughly as theology was shaping it. To go further back in history: Rev. Jonas Clarke was a patriot preaching patriot sermons. But if he hadn't been, he probably wouldn't have lasted a half century in Lexington's pulpit. In the largest sense, an established religion—whether official, like the Church of England, or unofficial, like the Protestantism Eisenhower named as America's "firm foundation"—baptizes whatever is around it. It can't really exist as an independent force; it's as trapped in its role as those red-coated soldiers marching down the middle of the road into Lexington. Their firepower is immense, but entirely predictable. They have no freedom of maneuver. When an institution gets very big, it's radical edge is very far from its center. And for Christianity that radical edge is actually the heart—or should be.

And so it's worth imagining (at least if you're part of the dwindling band still interested in the cross) what a nimbler small-c church might look like. Whether, to stretch the analogy, there's a possibility of a (nonviolent) Minuteman Christianity arising, one that's more flexible, more rooted, and *more dangerous* in the best sense of the word. A Christianity that might—in the new justice moment, the opening that appeared after the murder of George Floyd and as the planet overheats—play a useful role. Not a decisive role, but a useful role. I'm going to spend the rest of this section exploring that possibility, understanding that for some people it won't be of great interest: you're welcome to skip a few thousand words ahead to the next big discussion, about prosperity. But for those who are curious, let me say at the outset: I'm not in the slightest bit sad about where we find ourselves; if I have a nostalgic affection for the church of my youth, it's like my recollection of the root beer floats at Howard Johnson's. All things equal, I'd rather find a food truck. And I think they're out there to be found.

ONE OF THE things that makes it hard to see this new landscape is that the explosion that went off in American Christendom was a neutron bomb: it left the buildings intact, while wiping out the congregations inside. Indeed, there are plenty of churches for sale, with entire websites devoted to selling them.

("Over in Ida, Michigan, you could get your hands on this stunning empty church, occupying a large corner plot in the heart of the community; the church and parsonage both come included in the sale price, which at just $110,000 makes this listing an absolute steal.") I've belonged to small rural parishes that had to close and sell churches—it's excruciatingly hard, because people were married in those buildings, and some were buried out back. That's one reason I'm so grateful that many more congregations are actually finding creative ways to survive. They're like the bookstores that somehow survived the onslaught of Barnes & Noble and Amazon; they've had to adapt in all kinds of ways, emerging with a very different sense of themselves and their role in the community. Diana Butler Bass has been the anthropologist of those congregations, deploying graduate students out across the country to look at fifty congregations from Seattle to Florida in an ongoing effort to understand how they've managed to stay alive, and in some cases thrive. "Although diminished in size and prestige, the mainline church often possesses an unexpected and underestimated vitality," she writes. Its congregants are often shy about even calling themselves Christians, she reports—one pastor she interviews says they're "more likely to call themselves 'Christ-followers': You can almost see them stepping away from Christianity in their reply. It's their way of saying, 'It's not what you think. I'm trying to do something different. I'm trying to be someone different.'"

One thing these congregations seem to share is an understanding that Americans need community now more than ever, even if they don't know it. The triumph of hyper-individualism

left a hole behind, one that people can't quite name but definitely feel. "What they need is the family," one Virginia pastor explained. "A different type of family. That's where I see my
mission." And of course that recalls the early, pre-Constantine
history of the church, a series of communities (in those days
quite radical ones, holding property in common). In congregation after congregation, Bass found that music played a crucial
role in bringing these communities closer together: "in mainline
churches across the country I listened to music from a dizzy-
ing number of traditions: African, Caribbean, Native American, African American, classical European, Celtic, jazz, southern
folk, gospel, American country, contemplative chant, rock and
roll, techno-pop, rap." But they also provided quiet—which, if
you think about it, is one of the rarest commodities in our over-
connected world. Permission to lay down the phone and con-
template, meditate, pray, was as welcome as a drink of water on
a hot day.

This sense of being a little apart from the world comes, I
think, as a relief. Back in the days I've described, when these
mainline Protestant churches contained fifty-two of one hundred Americans, they had to be all things to all people. The
power that came with that—what we'd now call "privilege"—
was attractive, but it was such limited power. *If you're the culture,
then you can't be the counterculture.*

And Christianity, or so it seems to me, is far better suited to
be the counterculture.

It took me a while to realize this, having grown up in that
suburban consensus church; I didn't quite understand what the

Gospels were about. When people describe spiritual experiences that change their lives, they usually have something dramatic in mind: a visitation, a hallucination, an out-of-body experience. I've had the occasional moment when the membrane seemed thin, but for me the first key encounter was more subtle and extended. One year, not long after I'd left my suburban home and suburban church behind, I decided to take an hour out of the middle of each day to copy out the Gospels by hand. I was twenty-one, just arrived at the *New Yorker* as a very young staff writer, and I would close my office door (in those days offices had doors, and no one at the *New Yorker* would have thought of interrupting whatever crucial literary production was occurring behind them) and open my Revised Standard Version and a cheap spiral-bound notebook, and just start copying. I don't know how it came into my head to do this—save for some image of monks by candlelight copying manuscripts with quills; it's not an approved spiritual practice as far as I know. But I'm glad I hit on it because it slowed me down. I'm a fast reader— you should see me scrolling through Twitter—which means I miss a lot. And what I'd missed, it turned out, was a full sense of just how unrelentingly radical the Gospels were.

Virtually every page was just a list of instructions, or parables, or occasionally angry demands that we live lives almost entirely different from the ones Americans were actually living. This was exactly the moment of Ronald Reagan's ascendance; the year I arrived in New York as a newly minted college graduate, he gave a speech a few blocks away to twenty-eight hundred of his donors explaining that his party—which had just carried the country (including Lexington) in a landslide—was "the party that wants to see an America in which people can still get rich," a maxim that for the next four decades came to describe all political parties. In the same speech he castigated those who wanted a "bargain-basement military," and indeed to the present day the Pentagon budget has just kept growing, to the point where we spend more than the next ten countries combined. These were the years when mass incarceration began, as we launched a "war on drugs" in an effort to combat "inner-city crime."

All that was popular, but it was also the literal opposite of the words I was copying into my notebook, and there wasn't anything subtle about it. Read the passages slowly for a moment, as if you've never heard them before (which you may not have).

"Teacher, which is the great commandment in the law?" And Jesus said to him, "You shall love the Lord your God with all your heart, and with all your soul, and with all your mind. This is the great and first commandment. And a second is like it, You shall love your neighbor as yourself."

Or:

"You have heard that it was said, 'An eye for an eye and a tooth for a tooth.' But I say to you, Do not resist one who is evil. But if any one strikes you on the right cheek, turn to him the other also; and if any one would sue you and take your coat, let him have your cloak as well; and if any one forces you to go one mile, go with him two miles. Give to him who begs from you, and do not refuse him who would borrow from you."

Or, this advice to the rich young man who came wanting to know how he should live:

"Go, sell what you possess and give to the poor, and you will have treasure in heaven; and come, follow me."

I wasn't exactly a rich young man—when my apartment was broken into that year, the only thing of mine that got stolen was a cardboard box where I stored my dirty clothes, which the thieves dumped out, repurposing the container to haul away my roommate's Betamax. But I knew that in the context of the city where I lived, and the world where I lived, and with the job I had and the degree that I held, I was rich. So it was devastating to read the next sentence: "When the young man heard this he went away sorrowful; for he had great possessions."

I'm not telling this story to say, "I read the Bible and became a good person." That is at best a work in progress, and I have far more possessions now than I did then. I'm not telling this story to say, "How ironic that Reagan had the support of Christians, since he wasn't acting like one." By these standards Clinton and Obama didn't act like one either. What I'm trying to say is: it is crazy to try and base a culture or a government on the Gospels because they are too hard. Insisting that you're doing so can only mean squashing—reversing—the clear meaning of the words.

But that doesn't mean that the Gospels can't be a potent force. They can be—but only an outside force. I've spent much of my life as an activist, trying to make big change so that we can head off the climate crisis. And in the process I've come to understand the difference between the inside game and the outside one. The former is important: you need people inside the system who can implement, compromise, push, pull. But the latter—the outside game—is more important. Because it's where you change the zeitgeist: all those marches and protests and essays and coalitions—that's actually how, over time, you change what the world thinks of as normal and natural and obvious.

And it's there that Christians—and Jews, and Muslims, and shamans, and people of every other faith tradition—can play a role. Not a decisive role, but a role, and an important one. As it happens, the day that I'm writing these words I've also been on multiple Zoom calls, with religious environmentalists around the world: Catholics from four continents who were divesting their dioceses from fossil fuel stocks; and Protestants, Muslims, and Jews who were organizing to bring people to northern Minnesota for massive civil disobedience against a proposed pipeline. I knew many of the people on the calls because for years building a religious environmental movement has been one part of my work. Not a dominant part—I've spent at least as much time with scientists, and with entirely secular youth activists. But a wonderfully useful part, because people of faith bring to the work a particular set of tools. (Christians, for instance, have a handy talent for forgiveness, which, believe me, is not otherwise a feature of political movements.) And they are grounded in something—those texts, say—that seems to give them sticking power. Every movement for human betterment that I know about depends on them, not as the prime movers (they usually aren't) but as an inspired part of the whole.

. . . . .

I HAVE AN illustration—an exemplar—for what I mean about
this move from institutional force to a force that challenges
institutions. It concerns Lexington, but also the place I went
after Lexington, and a man I encountered there. That fat college envelope that arrived while I was off painting walls in the
retreat center where Dr. King had planned the Poor People's
Campaign? It was from Harvard, offering me admission into
the class of 1982. Why I got in I don't know: I was rejected
from most of the colleges I'd applied to, my parents certainly
hadn't attended, and I was useless as an athlete. And I wasn't at
all sure I belonged—the day I moved my stuff into a dorm in
the Yard from the back of my parents' Plymouth, the first person
I encountered was the boy across the hall, who was wondering
aloud where in this city he might find a launderer capable of
starching his shirt collars. Since I didn't know shirt collars could
be detached, I wasn't much help.

It all turned out fine, however. I soon found a happy home
on the school newspaper, which came out six days a week and
hence could absorb a lot of energy, and I soon learned that the
university didn't place great stock in the specifics of my academic
career. (The gentleman's C was a necessity, so that the shirt-collar-
launderers of the world would continue to donate squash courts
and biology labs.) And I found my way to Memorial Church, or
more properly Appleton Chapel, the small and ornate antecham-
ber off the main sanctuary where morning prayers were held each
day at 8:45, a tradition that dated back to 1636 and the university's founding. These were not precisely the same prayers that
Bishop Hancock or Reverend Jonas Clarke would have heard in
their school days: after an anthem from the choir, changing in

and out of their robes in a flurry to get to class, there was a five-minute homily from someone, often as not an administrator, a rabbi, an imam. Only a few dozen students came on a good day, but for me it was the right start to the morning. And it let me get to know Peter Gomes, the Plummer Professor of Christian Morals, who presided over the church.

Gomes—who preached each Sunday in the large sanctuary, from an ornate flying pulpit that left him, as he sometimes remarked, "fifteen feet above contradiction"—came closer, in certain ways, to embodying that Eisenhower-era American religious consensus than anyone I've ever met. He had grown up in Plymouth, blocks from the rock where the Pilgrims landed, and he still lived there when not in residence at Sparks House, his official parsonage at Harvard. He came of age in the American Baptist Church, one of the Seven Sisters of mainline Protestantism, and indeed he returned to his home congregation briefly to preach after graduating from Bates College in Maine and from Harvard Divinity School. He was a proud member of the Old Colony Club in Plymouth, the "oldest active social club in the United States" (having formed in 1769, though a dispute between Patriots and Tories slowed things down during the Revolution), whose members celebrate the Fourth of July each year by reading the Mayflower Compact and loudly firing a cannon before repairing to the clubhouse. He was a trustee of the National Cathedral School, of Boston's Museum of Fine Arts, and of the Roxbury Latin School, founded in 1645 and the oldest grammar school in the country. He was a remarkable preacher—"I would say I don't have a silver voice," he told me once. "But I have a pewter voice. I am able to shape sounds and phrases to my satisfaction." The recipient of forty honorary degrees from American colleges, he was an Honorary Fellow of Emmanuel College, Cambridge, not to mention a Fellow of the Royal Society of Arts. He offered the prayer at Ronald Reagan's second inauguration as president, and then again when George H. W. Bush took office in 1988.

Complicating the picture somewhat, he was also Black.

I became acquainted with him, as I said, in the pews at morning prayers—there were few enough undergraduates in attendance that we stood out. And he oversaw a project I did as a senior on Latin American liberation theology. He indulged me, really, because he made it quite clear (a withering glance over the top of his spectacles) that he had little use for these radical theologians. (Certainly his friend Mr. Reagan didn't, as the Nicaraguan contras and the El Salvadoran army that he was funding were at that moment murdering many of them.) Truthfully, I think I enjoyed him the way I enjoyed other anachronisms at Harvard, as a reminder of its truly ancient history; when we met weekly to talk, it was in the ornate sitting room at his Harvard parsonage, balanced on antiques and drinking tea from a silver service. I would have been disappointed to have learned that his collars did not detach.

But then something happened. In 1991, about a decade after I'd graduated, ascendant conservatives poured lots of money into campus magazines across America, to counter the liberalism that prevailed on campuses even as that liberalism lost ground everywhere else in the country. Harvard's right-wing journal was called *Peninsula*, and in November of that year it published an entire issue devoted to decrying homosexuality.

The cover showed a pink triangle being shattered, and the fifty-six pages were devoted mostly to what we'd now call trolling. It urged Harvard to set up programs to help its students "overcome or control" their homosexual urges, which it called "pitiable." It contained diagrams purporting to show "possible pathways to a homosexual orientation." And, of course, it contained a lengthy religious argument, quoting from Leviticus: "You shall not lie with a male as with a woman; it is an abomination."

The next day, about two hundred students gathered in the Yard to protest the publication—it was by all accounts a fairly perfunctory affair, like many other campus demonstrations over the years. Then Reverend Gomes walked down from the steps of the nearby church and began to speak. "These wicked writings are hurtful, divisive, and most profoundly wrong," he boomed in that familiar pewter voice. "You and I are made in the image of God," he said. He added that he knew what he was talking about because "I am a Christian who happens to be gay."

There was, the *Washington Post* reported, a pause, as people made sure of what they'd heard, and then "a gasp of astonishment," and "then cheering so loud that he could no longer be heard. The student protesters jumped up and down, hugged each other, tossed their hats in the air. They looked like the winning team after the World Series."

From our vantage point in history, this declaration may not seem so remarkable. But for Gomes, in 1991, it took real courage, and it truly mattered; soon, his scholarly explication of the half-dozen Bible verses that seemed to condemn homosexuality (but in fact condemned rape and prostitution) became the ablest defense against religious bigotry, especially since they came from an otherwise unimpeachable source (one of Gomes's great friends was Billy Graham).

But I'm not telling this story for its small but noble place in American history; I tell it because the experience clearly freed Gomes. Not to live a new life ("I do not have a partner, I have never had a partner, and I don't expect ever to have one," he told the *New Yorker*. "I have been in love only once and that was with a woman whom I loved in principle but not in fact. I think I am vocationally called to the single life") but to preach a new gospel. To read the sermons and books that poured forth from him in the years that followed is to glimpse what can happen when religion escapes from the need to serve consensus.

His last and greatest book—he died at only sixty-eight, in 2011—was called *The Scandalous Gospel of Jesus*, and it opens with a pure distillation of his old self. "When I remember that the literal translation of the term *gospel* is 'good news,'" he writes, "I recall a wonderful encounter with her late Majesty Queen Elizabeth, the Queen Mother.'" One summer day a decade earlier he said, he had "found myself at divine service in the parish church in Windsor Great Park, where the royal family attends Sunday Worship" when in residence there. Afterwards, "to my great delight," he had been invited to join both Elizabeths at Royal Lodge, the Queen Mother's residence.

> There, in her one hundred and second year, she was holding court in the form of a splendid pre-luncheon party in a setting worthy of a Merchant and Ivory film, and eventually I was summoned into the royal presence.... Among other observations, the Queen Mother remarked on how excellent the sermon had

been. "Don't you agree?" she asked me, which is a difficult question for an honest clergyman to answer, so I did what anyone would do under the circumstances: I agreed. Then, with that world-class twinkle in her eye, the Queen Mother remarked, "I do like a bit of good news on Sunday, don't you?"

"To that declaration I gave hearty assent, for the great gift of Christian faith is the proclamation of good news even in bad or difficult times," he wrote. And then he proceeded to explain, over 250 pages, precisely *what* that good news amounted to.

The key, Gomes stressed, was to remember that "Jesus was not a Christian, that he did not know 'our' Bible, and that what he preached was substantially at odds with his biblical culture, and with ours." Preaching about "Jesus," or worrying about his role as personal Lord and Savior concerned with your sweater selection, was absurd: it was *what he had to say* that mattered, and what he had to say was a collection of "dangerous, even revolutionary, ideas, nearly all of which remain to be discovered and acted upon." The most basic of those ideas is that the rich are in a lot of trouble. As Gomes points out, churchgoers are more familiar with the Beatitudes ("Blessed are the poor; the Kingdom of God is yours") than with the lines that follow immediately: "But how terrible for you who are rich now; you have had your easy life. How terrible for you who are full now; you will go hungry!" The Gospel message, he insists, was fundamentally about a "reversal of fortune: those who were on top would be cast down, while those who were downtrodden would be lifted up." Ministers, he said, tended to avoid those passages when they could. ("We know what gives offense, which is probably why we spend so much time talking about sex and Jesus spent so much time talking about money.") Constantine, he added, "knew that the way to domesticate the incipient rival to his own ultimate power was to make the church comfortable and complacent; and that to do this, the radical edge of Jesus' preaching and teaching of the Gospel would have to be dulled," with the church becoming "an agency of continuity rather than of change, conformity rather than transformation." It is, he said, "no accident that although Jesus came preaching a disturbing and redistributive gospel, we do not preach what Jesus preached. Instead, we preach Jesus." In the book, he salutes the "so-called theologies of liberation in the most oppressed places on earth," which is very different from the tone he'd taken two decades earlier in our seminars; he argues for, at the least, affirmative action and actually for something that sounds a lot like reparations; he also plumps for a "newly defined social gospel" based on "the new and transforming definition of neighbor" offered by the parable of the Good Samaritan. "Proximity and kinship no longer sufficiently define who the neighbor is, and they no longer define those to whom obligations are due. The neighbor is the one who has opportunity to do good to one in need." In other words, Lexington really should have voted for that affordable housing when it had the chance.

The most poignant part of the book was perhaps his reflection on Martin Luther King: the annual celebration of his birth, Gomes wrote, was "a January embarrassment" because "we are reminded of how far removed we are from those great events, how much remains to be done, and how little will there is to do it. How naïve it seems now," he says, "to imagine that there was a moment within the lifetimes of many of us today when

it was possible to think of redeeming social sin by moral courage, and to do so under the leadership of a Christian minister
who believed that the Gospel of Jesus Christ had social, moral,
and political implications." For "a shining moment it seemed
to work," and then that moment closed, back in the decade I've
been describing, those 1970s of maximum suburban ascension.

MOURNING THAT LOSS is natural—those openings for justice
don't happen often enough. But time moves forward, and we've
got new openings for justice right now. Might the church play a
role in helping? Not as lead players, because as we've seen religious institutions no longer have that strength or that central
place in our culture, but as supporting actors?

To bring this full circle back to Lexington, let me introduce
one final character, a Congregationalist preacher named Dan
Smith. A native New Jerseyan, he went to Harvard Divinity
School, and his first job, in 1998, was as associate minister at
Hancock—that is, in the pulpit that stretched back to those
early preachers of the colonial era. I'd long since left town, but
my parents were still there, and they quickly befriended Dan,
who was indeed beloved by many: one of those people you could
tell on quick acquaintance was deeply, deeply kind. And so I got
to know him too, especially when my father died and he was a
bulwark for Mom. (I was there, in fact, the night that Reverend
Peter Gomes, who had been Dan's teacher at Harvard, preached
his installation service at Hancock.)

Early on in his tenure at Hancock, Dan got fired up about
Habitat for Humanity, leading a delegation from Lexington's

churches and synagogues into inner-city Boston to build homes for poor people. "I think we built two houses," he said. "I was proud of that work, but a couple of years in, it became clear that Habitat was not a vehicle for systemic change." So he got involved instead with a proposal to build low-income housing on the edge of Lexington, at the old state mental hospital that sat across the street from the warehouse for the retarded where I'd spent all those odd and difficult Fridays. "It was my introduction to organizing—to justice, not charity," he said. "Before I knew it we're walking down the street to the planning department, looking at the maps on the wall, looking for places to build thousands of homes. We were trying to build with that economy of scale." It didn't work much better than it had in 1970—despite many meetings, he said. "I don't think we moved the dial very far." When it came to regional planning that moved across town lines, "people in the suburbs would protect their privilege by arguments about historical preservation or environmental conservation"—you couldn't build housing for poor people because it didn't fit the character of the town, or it would fill a wetland.

As one might expect, the inaction began to chafe on Smith. He gave a talk in 2001 at one of the town's synagogues, on Martin Luther King Day, thanking its members for helping with Habitat projects, but suggesting that the time had come for much more. In a rich suburb like Lexington, he suggested, a "first language" of individualism had come to completely dominate the language of community. "You are here in a place where many feel entitled to good health care, a first-class education for the kids and an above-average house. . . . If there is any time left over in this work-spend cycle, some people *might* practice their 'second language' of community"—might volunteer. But "within this dominant ethos of individualism, people have very little moral obligation, outside of family and taxes, unless of course they feel like it." And then Smith told about some of the people he'd been meeting as he pursued more public housing—in particular, the Greater Boston Interfaith Organization, or GBIO, a mostly inner-city coalition of churches that grew out of Saul Alinsky's radical organizing efforts in Chicago. They fought for very concrete changes to improve the lives of poor people—at that moment, he said, they were building a thousand units of low-income housing in Boston, called the Nehemiah Homes, after the Jewish leader who had supervised the rebuilding of Jerusalem twenty-five hundred years before. "Though they've been slow to tap the resources in many of the suburban areas around, I've started to wonder if this organization might be our ticket" to get closer to King's vision, he said.

It didn't happen fast enough to keep Smith in Lexington; in 2004 (after performing Lexington's first gay marriage), he moved in toward the city, taking the pulpit of First Church in Cambridge (America's eleventh-oldest church), a congregation further along in that journey toward justice. He found time to co-teach Harvard's preaching course with Gomes, and also to serve as vice president of GBIO, which was winning important campaigns around criminal justice reform and affordable housing. At one point he interviewed his old mentor Gomes, who confessed that his preaching had changed and deepened over the years: too many churches, he said, were simply offering "a kind of therapy," or "a gospel of success." "I'm beyond that now," Gomes told him. "Life is short. Time is short."

Indeed it is—one fears that the window cracked open by George Floyd's murder or Joe Biden's election will slam shut again before we can get done what must be done, and that this moment will pass like the moments after the Revolution, or the Civil War, or the civil rights movement. One fears we'll go back into spiritual lockdown. But maybe this new, humbled, post-consensus church can play a role in keeping that from happening. "I remember once preaching a sermon about the flagpole on the Green that says 'birthplace of American liberty,'" Dan Smith recalled. "I was like, 'are you kidding me? When we are living these lives of considerable privilege?' But now, finally, at this moment of reckoning there's a chance for churches to do some of this. To reclaim those practices of repentance and truth-telling. To say, 'wow, we fucked up.' We've got to be able to love ourselves, have grace for ourselves so we're not paralyzed by guilt and shame that we fucked up so bad, so that we can speak the truth about the sins we've committed and omitted, and turn towards God and one another."

And if you're looking for straws in the wind, there's this: in 2018, Hancock voted to join the GBIO and help with its pro-gressive organizing.

And this. In the summer of 2021, a large-scale "religious census" conducted across America found that the number of evangelicals had plummeted—young people simply weren't embracing that legacy of hatefulness. And in fact the growth in the number of "nones" had stalled as well. Improbably, the ranks of mainline Protestantism had begun to swell slightly. Where we'd been 13 percent of the population in 2016, we were now at 16 percent. That's a long ways from the fifty-two in one hundred in Eisenhower's day—and thank God, because as I've said, Christianity works better as a counterculture. But perhaps it's a small sign of *something*.

In this case, perhaps, a sign that those of us raised in this tradition might consider recommitting, but to a creed more radical than we once imagined, in the hope that it could help with all the other fights that face us.

THE STATION WAGON

. . . .

What exactly *is* a high-end suburb? We used to call them bedroom communities, implying that they were places to rest before returning to the fray and churn of economic life. Indeed, there's very little visible productive activity in a place like Lexington—the town had actually banned light manufacturing in a referendum a few years before my family arrived. It wasn't like the shipbuilding port where my father had grown up in the Pacific Northwest—when he was a boy, the docks were busy churning out seaplane tenders and net-laying ships for the Navy in the wake of Pearl Harbor. My mother lived for a time in Pittsburgh as a girl, and so she knew the flames from the furnaces, and the layer of soot they deposited each day on everything around.

Lexington was different, obviously—but it too had an economy. In fact, the American suburb is perhaps the greatest economic engine yet devised. An enormous percentage of America's postwar economic might—of the winnings that came from global dominance after World War II—was devoted to a single project: building bigger houses farther apart from each other. Once they were built, they had to be heated and cooled; the distances between them had to be driven; and those vast spaces had to be filled with stuff. These tasks became central to the American economy. And at its root was the most essential product, real estate itself.

When we moved to Middle Street, there was an empty field

across the road: Idylwilde Farm, as the tract was known, was a forty-acre section that had supplied a farm stand run by the Napoli family since the 1930s. The elder Napolis still lived across the street and raised extraordinary tomatoes in a small garden; but the sons had sold the land to developers the year before we arrived, moving their farm out a ring or two farther in the suburbs to some town where, for the moment, acreage was less valuable. For a little while Lexington considered the parcel as a possible home for the kind of affordable housing voted down in that referendum; after that it was slated for a standard suburban subdivision. The first year we lived there it was overgrown farmland, and we rode our bikes on sandy paths through the old fields, stopping when we found strawberry patches still bearing fruit. The second year we lived there they poured the asphalt for Idylwilde Drive, a bending road that ended in the classic bulbous cul-de-sac: we built a jump for our bikes on the smooth pavement (good fun until, overly cautious, I put the brakes on in midair and bounced over the handlebars on landing). The third year they started to build the houses, and I can remember the sight of the foundations sticking up out of the scraped and muddy soil. At night the construction crew often left a single bouncy plank to walk if you wanted to explore, and we did. Perhaps we also harbored some early, unspoken anti-gentrification sentiment, because I remember that someone in my junior high classroom came into possession of a BB gun, and one afternoon we took turns shooting out the newly placed windows of the half-dozen homes being built along the street. Or maybe we were just idiots.

The houses, when they were finally finished, looked embarrassed, standing there without a tree in sight, save for a few saplings carefully anchored in small circles of bark mulch. Each home, I remember, came with a carriage lamp by the front door, and soon most sported a basketball hoop in the blacktopped driveway. These houses weren't particularly large by current standards—a couple thousand square feet—but they were so new they looked plopped down from space. Most of them have since been greatly enlarged, and some of them are worth, according to the websites, $1.5 million, $1.6 million. Probably more by now.

That was what was happening out the front door. Meanwhile, behind our house, at the end of our skinny backyard, a small creek washed through a scrubby patch of forest. My brother and I built a tree fort there—when the maples were in leaf, you couldn't see our house. When we'd been there four or five years, that land too was developed. (It must have been about 1975, because this new cul-de-sac was called Bicentennial Drive.) We were past the point of shooting out windows, and a little more ecologically conscious: I was angered to see the stream dry up. Now, those homes are all "sun-kissed kitchen with granite," and run in the millions, too—look it up on Zillow. After that, new home construction near Middle Street pretty much ground to a halt because there was no land left undeveloped, and the three-quarter-acre zoning made it hard to subdivide. But not impossible. Where the regulations allow, backyards have sprouted a second massive home.

All of which is to say, we think of a suburb as a place without industry, but in fact the suburb is itself an industry, creating massive amounts of wealth through the building of homes and the escalation of property values. The total value of all the real estate in the United States is $33.6 trillion, or more than the

GDP of the United States and China combined. That spectac-
ular number helps explain, for reasons we've seen, much of the
racial wealth gap in the country. It also helps explain a great deal
about how America came to be a deeply conservative country,
and why most of the ice in the Arctic has melted. The only other
things in my lifetime that approach its economic impact are the
rise of the internet and the ascent of China. Understanding how
we lost that opening for justice in the 1970s, understanding the
rise of Reagan and libertarianism, understanding the failure to
grapple with climate change: that means grappling with the
sheer economic force of the suburbs.

Which is not easy; we don't necessarily want to hear it. In
fact, the first time I tried grappling with it, it nearly cost me my
(summer) job. I'd gotten unharmed through my assignment to
infiltrate the local Ku Klux Klan, and as a reward my editor put
me to work on what seemed a much calmer topic: an update
on the local real estate market. But as I called around to realtors, in those long-ago pre-Zillow days, I noticed something:
the average price for a house in Lexington in 1978 seemed to
have crept above $100,000. So I made that the lead of the story I
wrote, an article that was well read across the community. Especially by realtors, who were the most faithful advertisers in that
paper, and some of whom were soon reaching out in anger to the
editor. Not because the story wasn't true—it clearly was—but
because they were suddenly dealing with angry clients wanting
to know why *their* homes were still listing below that century
mark. I thought for a day or two I'd be fired simply to assuage
their fury, but I wasn't, because subscribers, almost as valuable as
advertisers, were clearly interested.

The realtors I had interviewed were, in fact, quite candid about how the town was changing, though most of them spoke anonymously. "They used to build a lot of GI housing," one agent told me. "But now nothing is being built except in the super-luxury class." Others described how the zoning kept out moderately priced housing: "I'm not sure that the society can or should support the current approach any longer," one realtor explained. "I don't think we should become that sort of town. The community suffers if it becomes more homogeneous. Parents worry about their kids, but their kids are in danger of becoming insulated." The problem, of course, was that that prosperity became a self-fulfilling prophecy. "Up until recently there's been a very liberal trend here," another realtor said. "But once they're in the boat and a property-holder, they tend to become more conservative." Another: "Those who were ultra-liberal tend to have mellowed." And: "This town has a reputation for being relatively progressive. But when push comes to shove, property values prevail. That's it in a nutshell."

That growing conservatism, rooted in property values, surely lay behind some of the political shifts of the era. It helped move America from Lyndon Johnson and the Great Society to Ronald Reagan in the course of just over a decade. It moved us as a nation from the expansive possibilities of the '60s to the cramped and grasping '80s idea that markets would solve all problems. I think it, more than anything else, was what birthed the hyper-individualism that has dominated our political life ever since.

. . . . .

LET'S TALK FIRST about those houses themselves, because above all that's what a suburb is: a collection of ever-bigger homes.

I explained before that the normal-size $30,000 house where I grew up turned, forty years later, into a million dollar house, simply by standing in place. But I didn't explain that that house no longer exists. While I was writing this book, it was demolished and replaced with a squat and massive structure, built to maximize the narrow footprint. It no longer looks like a kid's drawing of a house; it looks like a smallish junior high school crossed with a minimum-security prison. Since Google Earth hasn't yet debuted X-ray view, I can't tell you what's inside. But I can guess: I'd wager a Sub-Zero freezer that the closet in the master suite is bigger than my parent's old bedroom. (The *Atlantic* reported last year that closets had grown faster than any other part of the house—one interior decorator said her closet creations might better be described as "glamor compounds," designed so that people can display their clothes as if they were in a store, laid out on shelves under special lighting. It gives new meaning to the idea of "closeted," meaning turned in on one's self, hidden, private. Many suburbanites were turning their spare rooms into closets. "Guest rooms are nice, but your parents might come visit only twice a year. Your clothes, meanwhile, are a permanent resident of your home.") Across Lexington, at my old address, people compensated for the lack of new land by building on ever more of their particular footprint—lawns started disappearing as houses grew. The same general thing has happened across America: the average house is twice the size it was in the 1970s, even as the number of people living in it has steadily shrunk. A hundred years ago, the average population density of cities, suburbs, and towns in America was about ten people per acre; in the newest subdivisions we're down to about two people per acre.

Mathematics would indicate that with fewer people in larger spaces, they will come across each other less often—and indeed that sometimes seems to be the intent. Every year the National Association of Home Builders, at its Las Vegas convention, features an "Ultimate Family Home," and as suburbia kept booming, those homes got not just bigger, but eerier: major builders and top architects "began walling off space, touting one-person 'Internet alcoves,' locked-door 'away rooms,' and his-and-hers offices on opposite ends of the house. 'The new floor plans offer so much seclusion, they're 'good for the dysfunctional family,'" one builder told the *Wall Street Journal*. One year the dream home at the convention came with a personal playroom for the son, and the daughter's bedroom had a secret mirrored door leading to a "hideaway karaoke room," where a young girl could, one imagines, sing away her loneliness. Or not.

The privatization extends outdoors. Just last year the *Washington Post* reported that the "new American status symbol" was "a backyard that's basically a fancy living room." A builder reported he was constructing "125 decks a year at an average cost of $125,000."

"People want being outdoors to be as sophisticated as an indoor living room," another explained. Hence: "deluxe kitchens with cooler drawers, a luxury grill that rivals any stove in size and price, elaborate sound systems, and colossal, weather-durable televisions." Two-draft kegerator, semicircular fire lounge, infrared heaters, pizza oven. As one satisfied homeowner—who boasted more than a million views on Instagram—put it, "Why would you want to go to the beach when you can hang out on a beautiful deck with a TV, day beds, and refrigerator?" As the president of HGTV explained, "It's a natural desire to enlarge a home's square footage."

Mathematics again: there are only so many hours in a day, and those that are spent in private can't be spent in public. Even before the pandemic, the use of libraries had been dropping 3 or 4 percent a year for the last decade; the percentage of Americans going to the theater or to a concert had dropped; the crowds at pro baseball and college football were smaller than they used to be; even NASCAR was in decline. Everything that the affluent possess in private has swelled in size ("his dream deck included pool, waterfall, slide, hot tub, and grotto"), and everything that we share in common has been allowed to decay: that's what it means when we say we have an infrastructure crisis. Federal spending on infrastructure has fallen by half as a percentage of GDP since 1970; at the state and local level, spending is lower than it's been since the 1950s. And of course once this cycle starts, it's hard to break: an underfunded rec center looks ever less appealing compared to an overfunded deck in the backyard.

We'll discuss at more length how we got there: the story of choosing private over public has been the crucial philosophical shift of my lifetime. But for the moment it's enough to simply say where we are. On average, a suburban American lives in a bigger home, sharing it with fewer people. And on average they spend more of their time looking at a screen—most likely the smallish rectangle in their palm. The average American has gone from having three close friends in 1970 to two now. Only a quarter of Americans have managed to become friends with *any* of their neighbors. The average American adult hasn't made a new friend in the last five years. We consume more, and we do it more privately: that is what the suburban experience amounts to, in purely physical terms.

ALL OF THIS excess would matter somewhat less if everyone shared in it equally. And that seemed to be the promise of America in those years. Since the end of World War II, the country had grown steadily more equal: economists called that era the Great Compression, as wages rose quickly for employees, amid a boom that called for many kinds of workers. Lexington was part of this, albeit toward the upper end: its prototypical resident was an engineer at one of the computer companies or defense contractors that ringed Boston. (I learned to drive in the empty parking lot at Raytheon on Saturday mornings.) Meanwhile, some combination of high marginal tax rates for the wealthy (77 percent as the Nixon years began) and social norms left over from the Depression kept high earners in check. I read Tocqueville in high school, and his contention that "the whole society seems to have melted into a middle class" seemed to be an apt description of the America I was coming of age in.

As it happens, I graduated high school in 1978, which is the very year that postwar compression ended and the surge of inequality that has dominated my entire adulthood began. Most every year since then the gap has widened, till we've reached the grotesque cartoon we live in now, where the fifty richest Americans own more wealth than the bottom half of the population, 165 million people. (Between them Jeff Bezos and Elon Musk have more wealth than the bottom 40 percent of the country.) The average worker takes home less money in real terms than in the year I got out of high school.

If I keep referring to school, it's no accident. Many forces drove this rise in inequality, but one of them was an education gap that was beginning to yawn widely in those years. If Lexington lacked manufacturing—if real estate and consumption were its industries—it nonetheless produced a finished product: high school graduates, whose success in turn kept housing prices churning upward. When I was writing that story that nearly got me fired about rising real estate values, I spoke to one realtor who explained that not only did his agency list in their ads the colleges that Lexington High School grads would be attending, but "we mimeograph the letter the high school sends out each year about the number of National Merit Scholars this town produces."

I took all of this for granted, of course: I was dimly aware that the junior high school my class inaugurated was nicely appointed, but I had other things to worry about in junior high. I knew that some of the teachers at the high school were demanding, but it wasn't until I got to college that I figured out they were often more demanding than the Harvard faculty— which allowed me to cruise through four years in Cambridge, concentrating less on schoolwork than on the extracurricular pursuits (the school newspaper) that would land me a job on the *New Yorker* the week I graduated. That perfectly timed $30,000 investment that my utterly middle-class parents had made in a house in Lexington turned out to be a ticket to their financial security and to mine and hence to my daughter's, and yea unto the generations; five or ten years later they wouldn't have been able to afford it, and all our lives might have turned out quite differently. It's not as if I didn't give back. When I was a freshman in high school I helped found the debate team; my partner and I won the first state championship in the town's history, a title that the squad has retained each year for the last half century. And now, if you go and look at the real estate websites for Lexington, the "national awards for its debate team" are a prime selling point. It's probably my single most successful foray into wealth creation, all of it accruing to the people who happened to be living in those ten thousand homes within the borders of this one town.

Those borders mattered enormously. In 1973, the year after I started at that shiny new junior high, the Supreme Court issued a ruling I knew nothing about, in a case called *Rodriguez v. San Antonio Independent School District.* The dispute had begun five years earlier, in 1968, when students walked out of Edgewood High School to protest conditions. The school was overwhelmingly Mexican American, and it was a mess: since there was no air-conditioning in the summer, "all the guys carried handkerchiefs—you put them around your neck so you wouldn't sweat your collar, because we didn't have a big, large wardrobe." A teacher recalled winters without heat: water in the beakers in the science rooms would turn to ice. Restrooms were locked during the school day; teachers asked for railings to be installed along the stairs; the band wanted uniforms in the correct school colors. Ninety percent of teachers weren't certified, because they were cheaper to hire; the guidance counselors routinely told students to join the military, and indeed the district lost more students per capita in Vietnam than any other in the country. So four hundred students marched to the superintendent's office, carrying a banner that said "Everyone in America deserves a good education." Civil rights lawyers decided to test that proposition, suing on the grounds that per pupil spending in the city was a fraction of that in the surrounding suburbs. A three-judge federal panel ruled that indeed Texas's public school finance system, based as it was on property taxes, was unconstitutional—a ruling that, had it stood, would have turned education in America on its head. And then the case went to the Supreme Court.

The swing vote in the 5–4 decision belonged to a Supreme Court justice named Lewis Powell, who had just been appointed to the bench by Richard Nixon. Powell, who had served as a corporate lawyer for the tobacco giant Philip Morris and then was given a seat on its board, believed that the free enterprise system was under "broad attack" from the "college campus, the pulpit, the media, the intellectual and literary journals, the arts and sciences, and from politicians." The summer before his nomination to the high court, he'd written a confidential memo for the U.S. Chamber of Commerce that historians have since described as "a corporate blueprint to dominate American democracy," or a "call-to-arms for corporations." In it, Powell urged businessmen to unite with "careful long-range planning and implementation, in consistency of action over an indefinite period of years, in the scale of financing available only through joint effort, and in the political power available only through united action and national organizations" in an effort to build support for unfettered capitalism. (It notes that "the newsstands—at airports, drugstores, and elsewhere—are filled with paperbacks and pamphlets advocating everything from revolution to erotic free love. One finds almost no attractive, well-written paperbacks or pamphlets on 'our side.'") The key lesson was that political power is necessary; that "such power must be assiduously cultivated; and that when necessary, it must be used aggressively and with determination— without embarrassment and without the reluctance which has been so characteristic of American business." Powell was prophetic: following his advice, great industrial barons like the Koch brothers became our biggest political players; his memo belongs on any short list of the most important political documents in American history because it helped persuade American business not to compromise with the emerging demands of an awakening society but to build the institutions that would fight those compromises tooth and nail.

And in the short run Powell was perfectly positioned to strike his own blow against equality. He wrote the majority decision in *Rodriguez*, finding that the federal district court had erred when it demanded an end to the unequal funding for schools. Indeed, he said, if the ruling stood it would lead to an "unprecedented upheaval" in American education. He granted that "since, under the traditional systems of financing public schools, some poorer people receive less expensive educations than other more affluent people, these systems discriminate on the basis of wealth. . . . Apart from the unsettled and disputed question whether the quality of education may be determined by the amount of money expended for it, a sufficient answer to appellees' argument is that, at least where wealth is involved, the Equal Protection Clause does not require absolute equality or precisely equal advantages." It was enough, he wrote, that the children in the barrios of San Antonio had access to "education"; nothing required that that education be any good. "Any scheme of local taxation—indeed the very existence of identifiable local governmental units—requires the establishment of jurisdictional boundaries that are inevitably arbitrary," Powell maintained. "It is equally inevitable that some localities are going to be blessed with more taxable assets than others." That blessing must be allowed to stand—if it was eroded with respect to schooling, where would it stop? "How, for instance, is education to be distinguished from the significant personal interests in the basics of decent food and shelter?"

Writing many years later, the longtime *New York Times* columnist Nick Kristof called *Rodriguez* "the *Brown v. Board of Education* case that went the other way." (Indeed, Thurgood Marshall, who as a lawyer had argued *Brown*, was by then a Supreme Court justice himself; *Rodriguez*, he said, condemned "countless children [to] unjustifiably receive inferior educations that 'may affect their hearts and minds in a way unlikely ever to be undone.'") "If a single justice had switched, America would today be a fairer and more equitable nation," Kristof wrote. A little of the damage has been undone by state court rulings, where judges ruled that under state constitutions equalized spending was required. But the basic architecture of the educational sys-

tem stands—indeed, schools are in many ways more segregated
than they were in the 1970s, especially in regions like the Northeast, where zoning has preserved the suburbs intact. In fact, at
the very fine college where I teach, despite constant efforts to
diversify the enrollment, huge numbers of students arrive each
year from those same Westchester suburbs or, like me, from the
inner ring of suburbs Just Outside Boston. JOB, in fact, is a
recognized acronym, a testimony to what was once written in
mortgage deeds and Supreme Court opinions. We call students
whose parents went to the college "legacies," but in this sense
there are many, many legacies.

ONE THING WORTH noting about that court decision was its slim
margin. *Rodriguez*, like the other case I wrote about allowing
municipal referendum on affordable housing, swung on a single vote. Much of history is contingent—so imagine, say, that
Bobby Kennedy had not been murdered in 1968. (In one of
my minor Zelig moments, my mother told me many years later
that Sirhan Sirhan's mother, Mary, had been my nursery school
teacher.) Most historians believe that RFK could have turned
Nixon's narrow victory into a loss; there would have been different people on the Supreme Court; much might have been
different.

But history can also be fated, the product of forces far larger
than an assassin's bullet. I'm convinced that this decade of the
1970s, as it played out in suburbs like mine, exercised an outsized role in the fate of the country and the world, and so I'm

interested in figuring out just how contingent it was. Lexington, and by extension a lot of other places, could theoretically have swung in different directions. What tipped it?

Granted, Lexington was more liberal than most towns to begin with. I can prove it, because I spent much of the summer and fall of 1972, when I was eleven, working to elect George McGovern president so that we could end the war in Vietnam. The campaign set up a fund-raising office in the back of the Knights of Columbus hall; my mother would drop me off there, and I'd work for hours addressing envelopes—there was a time when I knew the postal code of every town in Massachusetts. (My heart broke just a little when the post office reorganized zip codes across the region a couple of decades ago.) Since my voice hadn't broken yet, the powers that be decided I was a little too young to be calling people and asking them for money, but they did let me stand outside the Stop & Shop every Saturday morning for three or four hours, selling McGovern buttons to shoppers as they emerged with their carts into the parking lot. There was one old man who, each weekend, tried to spit into my bag of buttons, but mostly the reception was so positive that I was psychologically unprepared for the outcome of the election, just about the most overwhelming defeat in American political history. My family humored me when I pasted a "Don't Blame Me, I'm from Massachusetts" bumper sticker on the Plymouth, and I took solace in the fact that Lexington had gone for the South Dakota senator over Nixon, 8,478 to 7,432.

Eight years later, Ronald Reagan racked up more votes than Jimmy Carter in the town; indeed, most of the suburban belt outside Boston turned red that year, and across the country the suburbs were the key to Reagan's landslide win. Something had happened over that decade, and it had happened where I lived while I was living there, and I'd like to understand it. It's time to actually talk about the station wagon.

WE DIDN'T HAVE one—we were a sedan family. But everyone else did: driveway after driveway filled with Country Squires and Pontiac Safaris and Buick Estate Wagons. The Silvermans, for instance, with whom we shared a double driveway, and who, on a warm summer evening, would pile all the kids in back and all the adults in front. We would drive off two or three miles to the Buttrick's ice cream stand, which happened to be on the very spot where a British patrol managed to detain Paul Revere on the way from Lexington to Concord. (Luckily, Revere had already recruited Concord doctor Samuel Prescott, on his way home from a date, and he spurred his horse over a low stone wall and managed to warn the Concordians what was coming.) When I say the kids piled in the back, I mean we crammed into the back cargo area—and, if memory serves correctly, on the back roads Mr. Silverman would actually lower the tailgate and let us dangle our legs over the back. Needless to say, all of this would now get you arrested for child endangerment, but we loved it. Loved it without thinking about it, because the car was the absolute unquestioned reality of our lives.

Americans had, of course, been buying cars in big numbers since Henry Ford started up his assembly line in 1913, but until the end of World War II the numbers were not *that* big: in 1950 there were only twenty-five million cars registered in the country. That summer, over Lexington, a fleet of seven skywriting planes puffed out a gasoline advertisement in the sky: "New Blue Sunoco," it said, day after day. The message took—all such messages took. U.S. factories produced eight million new cars that year, and by the end of the decade there were sixty-seven million cars on the roads of America. Those roads stretched everywhere, since the 1950s also saw the construction of the interstate highway system, the largest public works program in American history. I'd never left the continent till well past college, but I'd seen an awful lot of the United States: vacation meant piling into the car and driving, covering ground along the route that someone in the AAA office had highlighted in our Travel Guide, until about five in the afternoon when it was time to search for a motel. (The Travel Guide symbol for a swimming pool was an absolute requirement, and so much the better if the establishment boasted "Magic Fingers" technology to shake the bed when you inserted a quarter.)

It took no time—a decade—for America to construct itself around the car. That's what the suburb was, a reflection in concrete and wood and brick of the logic of the automobile, designed for its dimensions, its turning radius. Lexington was an older and more compact suburb, so it was theoretically possible to negotiate it without a car—but not really. We shopped at the mall one town over, and as far as I know no one had ever approached it on foot; why would you? And the further out you went, the more car-centric the suburbs became, just a series of branching roads that eventually turned into driveways. More than three-quarters of Americans drove to work, and most of them drove by themselves. As Meg Jacobs wrote in her history of the period, by 1970, Americans consumed a third of the world's energy—more than the Soviet Union, Britain, West Germany, and Japan combined. And mostly because of the car. By then there were 118 million cars and trucks on the American road—more than quadruple the number twenty years before. The cars were big: 20 percent bigger than they'd been just five years before. Three-quarters of them now came with air-conditioning (up from 20 percent in 1960), which subtracted about two and a half miles a gallon from the fuel efficiency, not that that was a thing anyone even thought about in 1970 because gas was 36 cents a gallon.

I got my learner's permit the day I turned fifteen and a half, and of course I sat through driver's ed, with its interminable film strips about kids who took a bewildering variety of drugs (bennies, greenies, Mary Jane, LSD, uppers, downers, quaaludes, coke, horse, angel dust—there seemed to be more drugs then, and they all had nicknames) and subsequently crashed their vehicles. (The classic movie showed a boy who, high on acid, believed he could control the stoplights with his mind. "For a while it seemed to work," the narrator solemnly intoned, but then it didn't; as I recall, the film ended with an image of his wrecked car being crushed into a steel cube at some auto graveyard—a cube dripping blood.) We practiced on a driving simulator, and then on the road with a baseball coach supplementing his pay—he directed me to merge onto the highway at seventy miles per hour four minutes into my driving career. I loved it, and not just because cars meant sex. (We literally called it "parking.") Because it meant economic freedom: you could work, in order to get money to buy gas.

But my work, as I've said, was for the local chain of suburban weekly newspapers, and the story that I covered more than any other was the sudden, violent collision between that car culture

and world geopolitics. I was too young to really pay much attention to the first oil shock in 1973, though I was aware that there
were suddenly long lines at Al's Gulf. But by all accounts it was
bad: at one Texaco station in town, the owner reported, "They've
broken my pump handles and smashed the glass on the pumps,
and tried to start fights when we close. We are all so busy at the
pumps that somebody walked in and stole my adding machine
and the leukemia-fund can." Nixon ordered a ban on holiday
lights—and even when he scaled back the order, businesses could
only put up about a fifth of the ordinary spectacle. The Daytona
500 was cut to 450 miles; one White House official traded in
his chauffeured limousine for a chauffeured Ford Pinto. But in
March of 1974, Saudi Arabia lifted the embargo that had trig-
gered the first oil crisis; prices stayed high, but life resumed: the
momentum of suburbanization hadn't been broken, though at
least for a while cars downsized—we never had anything quite as
long-nosed as that Plymouth Fury again.

    I was entirely conscious, however, when the second oil shock
hit, this time in 1978 after the Iranian seizure of the American
embassy. The gas lines returned, and I was covering them for the
local paper, making endless rounds of calls to local filling stations
to see when they'd be open and for how long, so we could print
the schedules on the front page. "Everyone is near 75 percent
allocation, which means one out of four people is not going to
get gas, and no one wants to be that one," the owner of the Shell
station told me. "I open at 7 a.m. and I'm pumped out by 11 a.m."
He was pleasant, anyway. "Hours? We have no hours," someone
answering the phone at Dom's Amoco snapped. "I pump gas
when I feel like it." In an effort to cut down the lines caused

by nervous drivers topping off their tanks, Massachusetts governor Ed King said motorists had to prove they had half a tank or less before they could pump; local gas station owners were unenthusiastic. "I don't think anyone in this business is suicidal," the owner of Steve's Service explained. "Sticking your head in the window and looking at someone's gas gauge is suicidal." One of my responsibilities was the police log, normally a fairly dry affair but now suddenly filled with reports of people arrested for siphoning gas out of cars parked in driveways. I interviewed school officials, who were busy repairing boilers: "Now they're burning at 84 percent efficiency," the head custodian explained. "That's better than most homeowners. We are stretching a gallon of fuel oil to its limits." And car dealers: "Big cars are dead," one VW dealer said. "The small cars are bringing more money than the big ones, even with all the goodies."

Along with gas station owners, I also got to interview the number three man in the country's energy department. John Deutch was an MIT professor, and in between Washington stints he lived in Lexington, so I talked with him the week before his boss, President Carter, was to give a nationwide address on energy conservation. Deutch—barefoot and in jeans on his back porch—was sounding appropriately sober. "If you're a person in a situation where there is too little oil, you would look for easy solutions and for scapegoats," he said. "But there is no quick fix. There is no question about the fact that until the American people understand that there is not as much oil as they want at prices they want, there will be problems." Carter had been striking the same note all along: in his first address as president he'd said, "We have learned that 'more' is not necessarily 'better,' that even our great Nation has its recognized limits." The energy crisis, he said, was a reminder that "ours is the most wasteful nation on earth." As the gas lines grew longer, his sobriety deepened. "All the legislation in the world can't fix what is wrong with America," he said. "Too many of us now tend to worship self-indulgence and consumption," he said, sounding different than any president had ever sounded. We should change—we should learn "that owning things and consuming things does not satisfy our longing for meaning . . . that piling up material goods cannot fill the emptiness of lives which have no confidence or purpose."

If that sounded like an attack on suburbia, well—it kind of was. Or, if not an attack, then an invitation to think a little differently. And an invitation that might, actually, have been answered. As I said before, there were close calls that could have gone the other way: Supreme Court decisions where a single vote would have led to entirely different worlds. And the same was true of much larger debates. The 1970s had begun with the publication of a book called *The Limits to Growth*, an argument that we were reaching ecological boundaries, which became one of the best-selling nonfiction volumes ever. A few years later E. F. Schumacher had produced *Small Is Beautiful*—a book so powerful that when its German-British author came to America, Carter hosted him at the White House. The sociologist Amitai Etzioni was a senior policy advisor in that White House, and he brought the president polling data to show how up in the air America really was; the data showed 30 percent of Americans were "pro-growth," 31 percent were "anti-growth," and 39 percent were "highly uncertain." That kind of ambivalence, he told the president, was "too stressful for societies to endure," and he was right—which explains, I think, the fateful 1980 election.

BY THE TIME that 1980 campaign was underway, I was in college, and firmly ensconced at the campus newspaper. Being Harvardians, and hence endowed with a terrifying sense of self-importance, we did not confine ourselves to covering events on campus—I spent much of that year in New Hampshire, following the presidential contenders across the Granite State. I chatted with Jerry Brown for half an hour in the back of his campaign bus, as he explained that before long we'd all have wristwatches that allowed us to read the news or send messages to each other (haha, I thought, what a flake). I crammed myself into the back of a rental car driven by John Anderson, a now-forgotten centrist whose surprisingly successful third-party candidacy would eventually help Ronald Reagan carry Massachusetts. And I was in Nashua the night that Reagan won the GOP primary by declaring, in a debate, "I paid for this microphone," an assertion of manly dominance that cowed his main contender, George H. W. Bush, and convinced a good many Americans that he was the answer to the "weakness" of President Carter.

Because it was such a watershed election, and because Reagan became such a towering figure in our political history, we tend to forget that two weeks before the vote Carter still held a lead in the polls—up 8 percent, according to Gallup, though the margin was shrinking. I sat down to write the final story on election night for the *Crimson* not knowing who would win—I was hunched over a manual typewriter and surrounded by spools of paper rolling off the Associated Press ticker as returns came in. I also had a case of Schlitz by my feet, and I drank as I wrote, grimly and methodically. My alcohol intake didn't, I think, affect the story, a shapely pyramid of facts about the defection of "union members, Midwestern and eastern voters, and even voters from Carter's own South," which left the Georgian as the first elected incumbent defeated since 1932. But by the time the story had been edited and the presses had begun to roll, I was as drunk as I have ever been, before or since, and I slunk back to my dorm where I slept for much of the next couple of days in a sad haze. Sad because—in an uncharacteristic burst of prescience—I thought I could see how the decades ahead were likely going to play out. How my lifetime was going to play out. As I slowly emerged from that beery fog, I made my way back to the newspaper, and, commandeering a small upstairs office, spent forty-eight hours producing a long editorial essay that, with the portentousness accessible only to college sophomores, I titled "Crashing."

Most commentators, I wrote, were blaming the landslide on dissatisfaction with Carter, but I thought it was "a near-total realignment of American politics." It wasn't, I said, the first such time in American history that the country had lurched to the right; we'd done that before, when obsequiousness to business had helped create the conditions for the Great Depression, and then thanks to FDR we'd recovered our equilibrium, a recovery that had now ended. But this time would be different—we were in a much tighter fix, simply because it was later in the human story. "To the scientists who predict that pollution, and over-production, and depletion spell disaster, the Republicans shout

'Pollution is From Trees.' 'There are New Sources.' 'We Can Get America Moving Again.' Just step on the clutch and put it in reverse." I knew they'd get away with it, because I knew that in the short run it would work. If you ended regulation, there *would* be a short-term boom in profits; if you stopped trying to share the wealth via taxes, it would for a time enrich enough people to form a working electoral coalition. "The American majority will sleep blissfully for the next 10 or 15 years—the years when our slide gains invisible but irresistible momentum—dreaming only of increased discretionary income." The alcohol had perhaps not fully worked its way through my system, because I ended with a dour if glamorous sense of how I should live the rest of my years: since perhaps "nothing would be enough" to overcome the forces now set in motion, maybe the only solace would be "a life spent trying, a life spent setting a non-violent yet non-compliant alternative to the irrational as it builds from every side and all around, a life fighting battles that can't be won."

It's a little hard to overlook both the condescension and the pomposity. (I was, in my defense, still a month shy of my twentieth birthday, which would be marked by a raucous party at the newspaper office, a celebration that would be interrupted when that same Associated Press ticker rang four bells to announce the assassination of John Lennon.) Still, I think my forecast was pretty spot-on. Reagan did lower gas prices, and in the process cement in place the notion that, as he repeatedly put it, "government is the problem, not the solution." That markets, left to their own devices, would solve all challenges. That our job was to get rich, each one of us. It was a notion that long outlasted him: His successor, the elder Bush, lost his job when he dared to renege on the idea of "no new taxes." His successor, Bill Clinton, declared the final end both of "big government" and of "welfare as we know it." His successor, W., cut taxes twice and sparked a housing bubble; even in the wake of that implosion, his successor, Barack Obama, with sixty Democratic senators by his side, didn't dare attempt a return to the days before 1980. "Through Clinton and even through how I thought about these issues when I first came into office, I think there was a residual willingness to accept the political constraints that we'd inherited from the post-Reagan era," Obama told the journalist Jonathan Chait in 2020. "Probably there was an embrace of market solutions to a whole host of problems that wasn't entirely justified." Obama's successor, of course, was the logical extension of Reagan, the cartoon version that thankfully lacked the political talent of the original, and hence surrendered the suburbs in 2020, giving us Joe Biden. Who, finally, with the crucial help of figures like Bernie Sanders and Elizabeth Warren, is making the attempt to get us past the 1980 election. But it is very late now.

And as for me, and the "life spent fighting battles that can't be won"? By decade's end I'd written the first book for a general audience about what we then called the greenhouse effect, and indeed that fight took over my life. I've been to jail more times than I ever could have imagined, and I have helped organize giant marches around the world—and half the sea ice in the Arctic has melted, fires ravage every temperate forest, and millions of climate refugees are already on the move, fleeing ever angrier seas and ever deeper droughts. I haven't given up yet—

the last part of this book will prove that—but it's been a long four decades.

BEFORE WE GET to the question of what we can still do to repair some of the injustice and salvage some of the future, I want to make the case that it didn't need to be this way. Had we broken the other way in the years I've been describing—had Carter's polling lead held, had we not insisted on tax cuts, had we made the choice to try and solve our problems less with individual solutions than with joint efforts—we might have ended up in a very different place. If we understand what that different place would have looked like, then we'll be able to calculate how much damage we did by choosing our actual course.

Let's think about inequality first, because that's what economists tell us may be our greatest woe. And not just economists: the epidemiologists tell us that the rise in economic inequality produced greater numbers of prisoners and school dropouts, more pregnant teenagers and drug users, far more mentally ill and obese people. As one set of researchers put it, "people in less equal societies are less likely to trust each other, less likely to engage in social or civic participation, and less likely to say they're happy."

So we should be grateful that a pair of researchers at the Rand Corporation think tank ran the numbers in 2020. They looked back to those years when I was in high school, the years when inequality was still narrowing in America, and asked: What if that trend had just continued? What if we'd kept adjusting public policy so that everyone's income merely kept growing at the same rate as the economy as a whole? If we'd done that, then right now the aggregate annual income of the bottom 90 percent of Americans would be about $2.5 trillion higher. Or, more plainly, every single American in the bottom 90 percent would be getting an additional $1,144 a month. Every *month*. Year after year. If you add it all up over all those decades, it amounts to a total of more than $50 trillion. As David Rolf, a union organizer, put it, "Are you a typical Black man earning $35,000 a year? You are being paid at least $26,000 a year *less* than you would have had income distributions held constant. Are you a college-educated, prime-aged, full-time worker earning $72,000? ... Rising inequality is costing you between $48,000 and $63,000 a year." At the median American income, workers would be getting more than $10 an hour extra income. "Even at the 90th percentile, a college-educated full-time worker making $191,000 a year is earning less than 78 percent what they would have been had inequality held constant."

The standard conservative reply to numbers like these is: so what? The tax cuts that fed the inequality produced gushers of extra money, so the unfairness is worth it: you're getting a smaller piece of a radically bigger pie. But, as economists have long since concluded, that's simply a lie; tax cuts *didn't* goose the economy the way they were supposed to. Reagan cut the top tax rate from 70 percent to 29 percent, and it's only gone lower since: Trump's 2017 tax cuts took it down to 25 percent. But economic growth in the 1970s—those chaotic years of oil shocks—averaged 2.92 percent; in the Reagan 1980s that growth jumped to, um, 3.05 percent. Trump promised that his tax cuts would be "rocket fuel for the economy," and Mitch McConnell insisted that "after eight straight years of slow growth and underperformance,

America is ready to take off." But, in fact, economic growth after the tax cuts was 2.92 percent, which is what it had been the year before.

"Our focus is on helping the folks who work in the mailrooms and the machine shops of America," Trump told supporters in the fall of 2017. "The plumbers, the carpenters, the cops, the teachers, the truck drivers, the pipe fitters, the people that like me best." But of course that didn't happen either—most of the tax cuts went to the very rich, and in 2018, for the very first time, the four hundred wealthiest Americans paid a lower tax rate than *any other group*. Reaganism had steadily, grindingly reduced itself to a sad absurdity.

Now consider the even deeper crisis of climate change, a crisis that presents the planet with a nontrivial chance that our civilizations could simply collapse in the decades ahead. What might we have done differently in the 1970s, even before we really understood the danger that carbon dioxide was posing? It turns out that in those oil shock years the Carter administration fixed on one key solution: massive government support for developing solar power. "A strong solar message and program," the president's domestic policy advisor Stuart Eizenstat told him, "will be important in trying to counter the hopelessness which polls are showing the public feels about energy. I'm quite convinced Congress and the American people want a Manhattan-type project on alternative energy development." Carter agreed to the plan—indeed, he said a *fifth of the country's energy should come from solar power* by 2000. He called for spending a billion dollars in fiscal year 1980 to create a Solar Bank, to fund research, and to provide homeowners with loans for putting up panels. He officially declared May 3, 1978, as

Sun Day, calling "upon the American people to observe that day with appropriate activities and ceremonies that will demonstrate the potential of solar energy," and directing "all appropriate Federal agencies to support this national observance." He observed this first solar holiday by traveling to a mountaintop in Golden, Colorado, home to a federal solar research facility: "The question is no longer whether solar energy works," he told a crowd (in a driving rain). "We know it works. The only question is how to cut costs so that solar power can be used more widely and so that it will set a cap on rising oil prices. In many places, solar heating is as economical today as power from nonrenewable sources." He added, "Nobody can embargo sunlight. No cartel controls the sun. Its energy will not run out. It will not pollute the air; it will not poison our waters. It's free from stench and smog. The sun's power needs only to be collected, stored, and used."

And then a year later he did something even more important: on June 20, 1979, he invited dignitaries and reporters onto the roof of the White House to watch the installation of thirty solar hot-water heating panels. "A generation from now," he said, "this solar heater can either be a curiosity, a museum piece, an example of a road not taken, or it can be a small part of one of the greatest and most exciting adventures ever undertaken by the American people."

In truth, it took much less than a generation to deliver the verdict: literal museum piece. Shortly after taking office, Reagan cut the renewable energy research budget by 85 percent and let the tax credits for solar panels expire; he did away with assistance for weatherizing homes and ended energy efficiency requirements for appliances; his national security advisor, Richard Allen, circulated an article insisting that the solar "energy crusade was little more than a continuation of the political wars of a decade ago by other means. . . . Where salvation was once to be gotten from the Revolution, now it will come from everyone's best friend, the great and simplistic cure of all energy ills, the sun." Instead, Reagan pushed hard for increased oil drilling in the United States, and for making sure that no pesky regulations got in the way. "First, we must decide that 'less' is not enough," he said. "Next, we must remove government obstacles to energy production. . . . Putting the market system to work for these objectives is an essential first step for their achievement."

And so in 1986 the Reagan administration took the panels down from the White House roof and stored them away in a Virginia warehouse. A top White House official—the *Washington Post* speculated it was U.S. Attorney General Edwin Meese—thought the equipment was a "joke." An official spokesman said, "Putting them back up would be very unwise, based on cost."

As it happens, I know a little about those panels. They were rescued from that Virginia warehouse by a faculty member at Unity College, a small school in a very rural corner of Maine, where for years they sat on the roof of the cafeteria, heating the water used in the kitchen. The college gave away or sold a few of them: I learned about them in 2008 when I visited the Sun-Moon Mansion, the headquarters of China's largest solar hot-water company. Huang Ming, who'd founded the company, kept one of Carter's panels in a place of honor in a small museum of renewable energy just off his executive offices. The panels, he said, had helped inspire him to create a business that was currently heating the water for a quarter billion of his countrymen—some Chinese cities, viewed from the air, look as if every single building has a solar hot-water heater on top.

Anyway, Unity officials agreed to hand me a couple more of the historic panels, and so in 2010 I rented a van, hitched a trailer behind it, and began dragging them south toward the White House. It was a fun road trip—three students and a professor from Unity were along, so there were iPod playlists and lots of snacks. We hosted rallies in Boston, New York, and Baltimore—we'd pour a gallon of water in the top of the heater, point it at the sun, and eight or nine minutes later steam would be churning out: thirty-one years later these things worked as well as they did the day they went up. Our hope, of course, was that Barack Obama (whom we all had worked to elect) might symbolically reinstall one, up top of his new house. We thought it made sense: when the First Lady had planted the White House garden a year before, seed sales had gone up 30 percent. We thought that the gift might help the administration restart solar history after three decades.

But no. Arriving in Washington, we were directed by administration officials to a side door at the Executive Office Building—the five of us were ushered by an intern in a blue blazer into the wood-paneled room where, once, the UN Charter had been drafted. This day, a trio of what the *New York Times* called "midlevel White House" officials met with us, in the single most frustrating example of bureaucratic obstruction I've ever gotten to witness close up. First they filibustered—long boilerplate explanations of how the administration was "building a bigger, better, smarter electric grid, all while creating new sustainable jobs." I sat back and let the three students respond, and they were magnificent: "Thank you for your good work," they said politely, over and over. "But no one really knows about it—certainly not our friends, who voted for Obama but are increasingly disillusioned. What better way to spread the word about what you're up to than the high-profile move of putting solar panels back on the roof?" No, said the officials, but they refused to say why. Literally refused. The students asked, again and again, and the woman who was leading the conversation kept repeating the same phrase: "If reporters call and ask us, we will provide our rationale." But they wouldn't provide it to us, and they wouldn't pose for a picture with the students, and they wouldn't accept the old panel even to put in storage.

Eventually we were back on the sidewalk, and the three college students were talking to reporters. They were in tears—of disappointment, but also I think of genuine perplexity. Amanda Nelson: "I didn't expect I'd get to shake President Obama's hand, but it was really shocking to me to find out that they really didn't seem to care. They couldn't even give us a statement." Elliott Altomare: "We went in without any doubt about the importance of this. They handed us a pamphlet." Measured the way activists measure things, it was entirely worth it: three stories in the *Times*, plenty of other coverage. We'd moved the needle a little further along. But I felt a little guilty about disillusioning these three students: they'd seen early on some of the cowardice and moral compromise inherent in holding power. And—for all my advanced years—I felt a little disillusioned too. It certainly made it easier to come back to the White House the next year and help organize the mass arrests on that same street corner that marked the start of the national fight over the Keystone XL Pipeline. In time we won that battle: we forced Obama to block KXL, the first loss of that kind Big Oil had ever suffered. And in time—safely into his second term—Obama did indeed put solar panels up on the White House roof. "The project, which helps demonstrate that historic buildings can incorporate solar energy and energy efficiency upgrades, is estimated to pay for itself in energy savings over the next eight years," a spokesman said.

In retrospect, it was pretty clear why Obama wanted nothing to do with those solar panels: they were tainted by their association with Carter. The 1980 election, thirty years later, still dominated our politics. We'd made a choice then, and that choice still held sway, even in the administration of our first Black president, a man who on the night of his nomination had said "this [is] the moment when the rise of the oceans [begins] to slow and our planet [begins] to heal." But he calculated that we hadn't yet reached the moment when we could move past that earlier moment in our political history. Read the quote from Obama again that I printed a few pages ago: "Through Clinton and even through how I thought about these issues when I first came into office, I think there was a residual willingness to accept the political constraints that we'd inherited from the post-Reagan era," he said. "Probably there was an embrace of market solutions to a whole host of problems that wasn't entirely justified." Probably.

. . . . .

INSTEAD OF MOVING toward solar energy in the Reagan years, we stepped on the gas pedal—literally—in our lifestyles, and on the brake—metaphorically—in the drive for something like social justice. Let's return for a moment to those years and that place: the suburbs at the end of the 1970s. Reagan's election wasn't the only sign that the close battle between progress and regress was breaking the wrong way. In 1978, California voters backed Proposition 13, which sharply limited the ability of cities and towns to assess taxes. Local property tax revenues dropped 60 percent overnight, and though the state filled some of the gap, services like education suffered immediate hits from which they never recovered: "They immediately dropped summer schools and adult education," Michael Kirst, who ran the state board of education when Prop 13 passed, told KQED on the fortieth anniversary of the vote. "Then they cut vocational education and counseling. They cut maintenance, assistant principals, librarians." Denise Saddler was a teacher in the Oakland schools: "Prior to Proposition 13 we had a robust music program, we had funded libraries—there was also a city library in every neighborhood that was open all the time and had summer programs," she said. "There were a lot of after-school programs for kids. There were many more opportunities." When the law passed, California was fourteenth in the country in per-pupil spending, and its schools were "the most envied public education system in the world"; now it's almost at the bottom of the national list, vying with Louisiana and Mississippi to see who can spend the least on its kids. "Many schools do not have a full-time nurse or counselor. In many of the poorer neighborhoods—in south LA, or the north-eastern San Fernando Valley—the library opens rarely. Janitorial service has become so spotty that some teachers have resorted to buying their own cleaning supplies and going over their own classrooms with rags and a mop at the end of a long day."

Not surprisingly, well-off families send their kids to private schools: enrollment has gone up by half since Prop 13 passed. Not surprisingly, the returns from the tax revolt went mostly to older white homeowners—half the property tax relief went to the 15 percent of households earning over \$120,000 a year—and not surprisingly the effects fell on the poor, who were mostly Black and brown. Indeed, Howard Jarvis, the politician who pushed hardest for its passage, explained that illegal immigrants "just come here to get on the taxpayers' gravy train."

Massachusetts passed its own version of the law in 1980, the same night that Reagan triumphed, and it did so with the support of suburban communities, including Lexington. There were other signs of the times too: a plan to extend the Red Line subway out of Boston to Lexington, for instance, died in this same period. There were the usual noises about congestion and parking—but there were also plenty of residents who didn't like the idea that "people from the city" would, for the mere price of a token, be able to arrive in the center of their town.

And so nothing changed while everything changed. Yes, the town now votes reliably liberal again—indeed by far wider margins than in the McGovern years. Biden got 16,308 votes to Trump's 3,337—but so what? The damage has long since been done.

We are, perhaps, finally starting to move forward again, as Joe Biden tries to pass laws that extend real benefits to the poorest people, and as the racial reckoning that followed George Floyd's murder perhaps—perhaps—moves us to rethink policing and punishment. In California, for instance, COVID relief funds are being spent on public education, and the state will soon have pre-K classes and two school meals a day for all students, moving it back toward the forefront of national educational standards. The traditional view is that this is how it works: change comes in fits and starts. Here's Obama again (I keep quoting him because he's by far our most thoughtful modern president on the meaning of progress): "That's been the history of America. Right? There is abolition and the Civil War. And then there's backlash, and the rise of the KKK. And then Reconstruction ends, and Jim Crow arises. And then you have a civil rights movement, a modern civil rights movement and desegregation. And that, in turn, leads to pushback and, ultimately, Nixon's Southern strategy. And what I take comfort from is that in the traditional two steps forward, one step back, as long as you're getting the two steps, then the one step back is the price of doing business."

The point I want to make is: that's too easy. In the long pause between steps forward as a society, some of us were making big steps forward as individuals. Other people are further behind than they were before. It's not just that we didn't pay down historical debts; it's that those debts grew much, much larger. The *Wall Street Journal* calculated in 2021 that the median net worth for Black households with college grads had fallen to $8,200, compared with $114,000 for their white counterparts. The interest compounded.

It's easiest to see this compounding debt, perhaps, if you look at the question of climate change. Imagine if we'd followed Carter's lead and actually done the work to make sure that by

2000 the United States was running on 20 percent solar energy. It would have been hard as hell—hard as the Apollo project, or the Manhattan Project that Carter referenced when he made the proposal. But the technological breakthroughs that came in the 2010s would have come in the 1990s, in time for China to adopt them as it began its epic economic acceleration. Our use of fossil fuels would have peaked decades ago, and the rest of the world would have followed in train. The carbon curve would have been bent decades earlier. We wouldn't have avoided some measure of global warming: momentum would have carried us past 350 parts per million carbon dioxide in the atmosphere, the level that scientists identified as the red line for climatic disruption. But not so far past, and not so fast. Climate change would have turned from an existential crisis into a manageable problem on a list of other problems.

Instead we did just the wrong things, nationally and individually. We ended most regulation for the fossil fuel industry, and so that industry went on a spree, producing ever more oil and ever more profit. And as it did so, its political power only grew. We now know that it used that power to build a massive campaign of climate denial and disinformation, one that derailed efforts here and abroad to do anything about the emerging threat. The CEO of Exxon, for instance, on the eve of the first global climate talks in Kyoto, flew to China and gave a speech telling that nation to go full speed ahead with fossil fuel development: the planet, he said, was cooling. His mendacity cost him nothing: indeed, a year later, with the election of George W. Bush, the oil companies gained unprecedented access to the White House, meeting secretly with the vice president to set energy policy. Under Obama, America passed the Saudis and Russians to become the biggest producer of hydrocarbons on planet Earth—he boasted to an Oklahoma audience that "we've quadrupled the number of operating rigs to a record high. We've added enough new oil and gas pipeline to encircle the Earth and then some." (Out of office, he told a crowd of cheering Texans that oil production "went up every year I was president. That whole, 'suddenly America's like the biggest oil producer and the biggest gas,' that was me, people.") As with all things, Trump took it to the furthest possible extreme: climate change was a hoax, windmills cause cancer. Days after his election he promised, "I will cancel job-killing restrictions on the production of American energy, including shale energy and clean coal."

Now, again, finally, we're trying to make positive change: Biden has canceled some pipelines, invested some money in renewable energy. Carter wanted 20 percent solar by 2000; if Biden's plans can somehow overcome the block that is West Virginia senator Joe Manchin (recipient of more oil money than anyone else in DC), we may get there by 2030. I imagine Lexington will be ahead of the curve. Town Meeting passed—thanks to wonderful activists at its Global Warming Action Coalition—a 2021 law requiring that all new construction in the town come with clean electric heating systems. The town acquired its first electric vehicles—a pair of Nissan LEAFs—in the fall of 2020, and I'm sure many more will follow.

But none of that erases what happened in the intervening forty years, the years when we piled up an almost unimaginable carbon debt. Year after year after year, people kept building bigger houses. Year after year after year, people kept buying more, and bigger, cars: the Country Squire station wagon turned into the

Denali, the Yukon, the Tahoe, all the mammoth machines named for the things that their emissions were melting or burning. It's not that people didn't know. Remember Dan Smith, the minister pushing fruitlessly for more affordable housing in Lexington? Twenty years ago I sat with him in an upstairs room at Hancock Church, painting posters for a protest outside Boston SUV dealerships the next day. His sign was inspired: "What Would Jesus Drive?" a slogan provocative enough that it spurred a movement across the country. But not a big enough movement to matter. The number of households in America with two or more cars went from about a third in 1970 to about two-thirds today, even as the number of people per household steadily fell. Lexington put in a small bus system, and a wonderful bike path, and yet the number of people driving alone to work remained at 71 percent in 2019.

And it was precisely those forty years that broke the back of the climate system, the years when we soared past the levels of carbon in the atmosphere that scientists have identified as the key danger levels. February of 1985 was the last year in which the planet had a cooler-than-average month; ever since then it's been hot. It's important to remember, always, that climate change is not like a normal political problem, because—just as with the gap in relative wealth between Black and white people—it compounds over time. To understand the distinction from our usual political woes, consider a non-compounding problem like health care. When I was a high school senior, we won the state debate championship arguing the topic "Resolved: The federal government should guarantee a comprehensive system of medical care for all Americans." We've made, at best, incremental progress toward that goal in the years since, and as a result millions of people have died or gone bankrupt. But when, eventually, we join the other industrialized nations of the world and decide to guarantee health care to all, our failures in 1980 or 1990 or 2000 or 2010 won't make that job harder.

The compounding problems are different. Each year that the wealth gap persists untended, it gets worse: if I have more assets, those assets make more assets. And each year that we keep burning fossil fuels we add to the load of carbon in the air—that CO_2 molecule persists in the atmosphere for more than a century, trapping heat the whole time.

So the exhaust from the Navigator or the Escalade that traveled a smooth paved road to the Stop & Shop in 1994 will still be there altering the climate at the end of this century. The 2012 upgrade to a sixty-inch flatscreen required more electricity, and the carbon that came from the smokestack of the gas plant that produced that juice is even now, silently, trapping the heat that is turning some ice floe off Baffin Island into seawater. Oh, and when it melts that nice white ice into blue seawater, it changes the albedo—the reflectivity—of the earth, causing it to absorb more of the sun's heat, thus amping up the whole process. These were the years that took us past the tipping points: in 1981 and 2003 and 1987 and 1993 and 2014 and 2008 and 1999 and every other year along the way, Americans, per capita, were pouring carbon into the atmosphere faster than any other people on earth, and in 2024 and 2037 and 2081 and for that matter in 2456 people (and other species) are going to be paying the price. The choices we made in those years around 1980 will turn out to be more important than any choices any nation ever made—they'll be visible in the geological record long after everything else about us is forgotten. If you think the Confederates left a lot of obnoxious monuments scattered around the country (and they did), well: the forest fires and floods are *our* monuments. Driving a Tesla today can perhaps keep that debt from worsening, but it can't erase it.

HOW MUCH DO we owe, exactly?

Right around the turn of the millennium, I took a reporting trip to Bangladesh. I'd already been working on global warming for more than a decade, and so I knew all the science and statistics. But we were still at the stage where the visible damage was just starting to crawl out of the cocoon of conjecture, and I figured Bangladesh would be a good place to look because on the scale of vulnerability it ranks off the charts. It's a river delta, so the whole country is low to the ocean, and as the seas rose on the stormy Bay of Bengal, prime farmland was already being eaten away. Meanwhile, the upstream glaciers that feed that delta with the waters of the Brahmaputra are melting; when they disappear, so will the country's geologic reason for being. I was poking around the countryside and falling in love with the place and its people: Bangladesh still has an intact rural peasant economy, something that has disappeared in most of the world as industrial farming has taken over, and so I'd wandered happily from one village to the next, chatting with people about their rice crops or the jackfruit harvest.

While I was there, however, the country's chronic climate crisis suddenly presented itself in acute form: the capital city, Dhaka, had its first big outbreak of a disease called dengue fever. The scientists at the World Health Organization have called dengue "the emergent disease" of this century because the mosquito that spreads it—*Aedes aegypti*—is overjoyed at the warm, wet world that we've been constructing. Dengue is ugly. A normal case lays you low for a week or two with a debilitating fever and excruciating pain in the joints (it used to be called "breakbone fever"). A bad case—often a second case—can turn hemorrhagic, and you can bleed from various orifices until you die. So people in Dhaka took the outbreak very seriously: the front page of the paper ran hugely magnified drawings of the mosquito that carries it, and the city sent out workers to turn over buckets and coconut shells to drain the standing water where the insects breed. But it was a daunting task: most of Bangladesh is standing water. And so the disease kept spreading. Eventually, because I was spending a lot of time interviewing people in the city's riverine slums (many of whom had been forced from their coastal villages by rising ocean levels), I got bit by the wrong mosquito. And I became very sick, as sick as I'd ever been: there were nights when if I held my arm out the sweat would pour off the end of my extended finger like rain down a gutter. The rash itched terribly, but I was almost too lethargic to scratch. And there was little to do: the clinic in downtown Dhaka had thousands of victims lined up on cots, but aside from giving people aspirin there wasn't any treatment.

As I looked at those cots, the actual meaning of climate change became clearer to me: it was, along with a practical threat, the most immoral thing imaginable. Since I'd been in Bangladesh for weeks, I knew viscerally what the statistics could easily ratify: no one here had done a damn thing to cause it. There were cars in Dhaka, but not that many: bicycle rickshaws were still moving people around the city. In the countryside it was feet, and ferries. In 2000, Bangladeshis emitted 0.2 tons of carbon per person; Americans emitted 22 tons per person, or about a hundred times as much. Bangladesh was a rounding error in the cause of its misery. America—much less miserable—was largely responsible. How largely? Americans have produced about a quarter of all the excess carbon in the atmosphere: the 4 percent of us who occupy this land account for 25 percent of the damage, and of course the higher up the ladder you go, the more you produce. Suburban Americans produce about twice as much carbon as their urban brethren. And how could they not? The entire layout of the suburbs—those single-family houses (and the zoning to make sure nothing else gets built)—might as well be designed to burn as much energy as possible. If there were a thousand cots in that Dhaka clinic, then 250 of them were the responsibility of us Americans. The math is pretty straightforward.

And again, of course, this damage keeps compounding too. So, for instance, a recent study found that each dengue case in Malaysia cost about $718 to treat, or about one-fifth of the country's gross domestic product. That's the equivalent of fifty-three days of lost economic output for each person treated, and so that means far less money to spend on HIV education or reducing maternal mortality or anything else that a health system should be doing. Year after year, decade after decade. And of course dengue is one of the more minor manifestations of rapid climate change. Every year disease spreads; every year drought diminishes harvests; every year money must be spent to contain rising sea levels until they can no longer be contained; every year storms wash across nations too poor to mount real defenses.

Think about 2020, the hottest year ever recorded on the planet (so far), and the year that saw (so far) a record number of tropical storms in the Atlantic. By the time the last of them crashed ashore we'd run out of the alphabet and resorted to Greek names—and we weren't paying much attention, because those November hurricanes failed to hit the United States. Instead, Eta and Iota spent themselves on Central America—the two vast storms hit ten miles apart and ten days apart, and together they did almost incalculable damage. The early estimates put the economic toll on Honduras at 40 percent of the country's GDP (by comparison, Katrina, the worst storm ever to hit the United States, did damage roughly equal to 1 percent of our economy). Farmers looked out on fields now covered with feet of sand; the roads needed to get their crops to harvest were gone, the bridges demolished. And so it is no surprise that many Hondurans decided to trek north toward our border. I don't know their legal status—refugee law has yet to catch up with the climate crisis—but it's not hard to calculate their moral standing: the last numbers I can find for Honduras show its citizens producing about a ton apiece of carbon dioxide a year, about a sixteenth of the current American total. If you want to know what wrecked the bridges of San Pedro Sula, look to the SUVs of suburbia. In the wake of the great storms, a *Washington Post* reporter found a woman named Blanca Costa crouched on a wooden cart with her three daughters—they were sheltering under a highway overpass after the floods had destroyed their one-room house. It had also killed the three horses that drew the cart, enabling her to make a small living collecting trash. "It would take years, she said, to save enough money to buy another one. 'I'll just have to go on foot now. . . . But it will be more difficult,'" she said. The impossibility of her life going forward is in some serious way related to the comfort of our lives in the recent past.

The firmest mathematical delineation of the actual size of this accumulated debt comes from an old friend of mine named Tom Athanasiou, who's been working on the climate crisis for nearly as long as I have. He runs a nonprofit called EcoEquity and has taken it upon himself—with collaborators around the developing world—to figure out what the fair share of carbon reductions for each country should be, accounting for both our share of emissions and the wealth we built up burning up that fossil fuel. At the moment, of course, the United States is pledging it will reduce its net emissions to zero by 2050, which is a vast improvement on Trump. But it's not the same thing as reckoning with our actual obligation. Our real responsibility, EcoEquity figures, looks more like this: "the U.S. fair share of the global mitigation effort in 2030 is equivalent to a reduction of 195% below its 2005 emissions levels." Obviously we can't reduce our emissions 195 percent—that's mathematically impossible. In fact, as Athanasiou points out, even on a wartime footing we'll have a hard time getting them down more than 70 percent in the next decade or two. So the other 125 percent would have to come in the form of cash, turned over to the people of the global south so that they could build both solar panels and sea walls. This translates into roughly $100 billion a year in international climate finance from the United States for each year of the next decade. Which sounds like a lot of money, but compare it with, say, the value of all the housing in the United States, which comes to about $33 trillion, and grows in value by more than $2 trillion annually. A hundred billion dollars is about a twentieth of that annual appreciation in value. We don't, actually, lack the money to do what justice demands.

WHAT WE MAY lack is the sense of neighborliness. For me, the scariest thing about the last forty years, even more than the rising temperature, was the ascension of the libertarian idea that the individual matters far more than the society an individual inhabits. The *New York Times* called Ayn Rand ("altruism is incompatible with freedom") the "novelist laureate" of the Reagan administration, and by the Trump era that affection had only deepened. Her "books pretty well capture the mindset" of the Trump administration, Trump's first nominee for secretary of labor explained. "This new administration hates weak, unproductive, socialist people, and it admires strong, can-do profit makers." Her literal acolyte Alan Greenspan ruled over the global economy as chair of the Federal Reserve for much of that period, and the basic tenets of the philosophy never wavered: Public is bad. Private is good. Watch out for yourself. Solidarity is a trap. Taxes are theft. You're not the boss of me. Reagan's big punchline, in hundreds of speeches over dozens of years, never varied: "The nine most terrifying words in the English language are: I'm from the Government, and I'm here to help."

That spell may finally be breaking now: the scariest words in the English language, it turns out, are "we've run short of ventilators." Or "the hillside behind your house is on fire." Or "I can't breathe." And they point to crises that can be solved only when we act together.

"Communal responsibility for the welfare of inhabitants" was a "prevailing ethic" in the early Puritan settlements like Lexington, historian Richard Kollen reports: the town account books from the early years show that it was "a very small welfare state," taking care of the neediest from cradle to coffin: "When Thomas Paul's wife died in 1728, the town paid for 'digging her grave' and for 'seven quarts and one jill of rhum for her funeral.'" The town "also operated an early form of subsidized health care, with the local physician charging the town rather than the individual for medical care." (The most famous bill came from Dr. Joseph Fisk, who charged the residents for attending the wounded British soldiers after the fight on the Green.) But if the town took care of its own, it also made sure that not too many people ended up on its tab: if people moved to Lexington or other communities who didn't seem likely to be able to support themselves, they were "warned out" by the town authorities—told to leave, or at least not to expect support if they stayed.

By this point in history, it's pretty hard to draw such lines: that's what the storms of Honduras mean. There are, relatively speaking, no poor people in Lexington: 5 percent of the children in its schools get free or reduced-price lunches. But there are plenty of poor people *outside* of Lexington: more than half of American students are enrolled in the free lunch program. And of course the next ring out after that encompasses the whole world—Dhaka, drowning. Honduras, wrecked.

I've argued in this book that there are a series of debts owed. The debt that we call reparations, for the systematic racial discrimination that let some people prosper and forced others to fail no matter how hard they worked. The carbon debt that leaves some people with three dead horses because others have three-car garages. Debts like this have grown enormously over these last forty years. And these debts call into serious question the meaning of the symbols we theoretically honor: What does it mean to raise that flag above Lexington Green, when the country it symbolizes has so systematically refused to engage with its history? What does it mean to look up at the cross atop the steeple on the church beside the Green, when that faith it symbolizes has so often embraced the mainstream culture and not the people at whom its message was clearly aimed? What does it mean to enjoy the unprecedented prosperity of the American suburbs when that prosperity now clearly comes at the expense of so many others?

I don't think that these things are beyond redemption, but I also don't think the redeeming is going to be free, or even cheap. Since America over these decades has been so wildly successful, the funds are available: that bank that Dr. King described has plenty of cash, and there is no need for the promissory note to come back marked "insufficient funds." Debts are there to be paid.

The remaining question is, who should pay them?

PEOPLE OF A CERTAIN AGE

. . . .

The stories in this book have mostly come from long ago, from the decade when I grew from ten to twenty. They come from the decade that began, for me, with that protest on Lexington Green when I felt—in ways I obviously couldn't have articulated, even to myself—that I was connected to a world standing up to unjust power. They come from the decade that ended for me with that beery despair on the night that Ronald Reagan won the presidency.

I'm not young anymore—I'm in my sixties now, the son of a father who was diagnosed with a brain tumor at sixty-eight and dead inside of six months. I've spent some of the intervening forty years doing what I could to—well, "better the world" sounds absurd, so let's just say I've taken some of the idealism from those Sunday school classrooms and those years telling the story of the brave minutemen, and I've taken the fine education that luck and geography and circumstance provided me, and I've used them to cause what trouble I could. I've helped launch big movements and block big pipelines and force big banks to change their policies; I've written many books and given so many speeches; I've worked on party platforms and gone to jail. I hope it's helped, but obviously it's not been enough; hence the traumas I've been describing, from the widening racial wealth gap to the rising temperatures.

I'd like to keep trying; in fact, I'd like to win some of these fights. And I think that one group that could help make that possible are my fellow Americans who also aren't so young anymore, the boomers and the silent generation above them. The people who grew up with the suburbs, the sexa- and septua- and octa- and nonagenarians, the people who feel like they have no time left to waste. (I even know a few centenarians who want to help.) Taken as a whole, these are the generations who have given us the troubled country we inhabit—the voters who gave us Reagan and then Trump, the people who kept the apartments out of the affluent suburbs and built the jails and bought the SUVs. But some of them have always dissented, and now I think it's at least plausible that a significant portion of this demographic is ready to act differently. Remember: the first act of these lives was fascinating. We participated in or at least bore witness to the last period of broad cultural and social change, to the civil rights and antiwar and women's movements. We saw the justice window open, and then we saw it close. The second act of our lives was, to again speak in generalities, more privatized—more focused on individual accomplishment, often to the detriment of the larger world. We were better consumers than citizens. But many of us are now emerging into our latter years with skills, with more than our share of resources, and with grandchildren. Surely that might give us the capacity and the reason to help. Not to lead: the leaders of work for change are younger people, who have risen to the occasion. But they need backing; they need our third act to improve on the second.

. . . . .

WISE PEOPLE ENTER any generational discussion with trepidation. Even if you can keep track of who constitutes Gen X and what are millennials and tween-somethings, it quickly becomes a graveyard of careful thinking. There are seventy-two million millennials and seventy million boomers—that means you're making generalizations about populations larger than France or England.

But everyone does it. I spent a couple of decades listening to my peers complain about the apathy of "kids today," and then— since I've spent most of the last couple of decades organizing with young people, who are not apathetic in the least—I've heard plenty of complaints about boomers. Younger people who (thankfully) would not dream of saying anything disparaging about any ethnic group or sexual minority are utterly uninhibited about their scorn for the class of older people. "OK Boomer" is the least of it: here's a writer named Gene Marks, who to judge from his Twitter account spends most of his time advising people about their 401(k) plans. But man, does he hate "our worst generation." In fact, the "only good news is that the baby boomer generation is quickly getting older. Ten thousand boomers are retiring each day. We can't ship them all off to an island, unfortunately . . . but we can soon bid farewell to that horrible generation."

The criticism comes from everywhere. From the right: in her book-length account of *Boomers: The Men and Women Who Promised Freedom and Delivered Disaster*, millennial Helen Andrews, the senior editor of the *American Conservative*, accuses boomers of being "fools"—of "inheriting prosperity, social cohesion, and functioning institutions" only to pass on "debt, inequality, moribund churches, and a broken democracy." The critique comes from the center: Bruce Gibney—venture capitalist and early investor in PayPal—titled his 2017 tome *A Generation of Sociopaths*, attacking the boomers for, among other things, not paying enough attention to crumbling infrastructure. ("There's something like a $4 trillion deficit in deferred maintenance," he explained, so add that to the list of debts.) And it comes from the Left: the millennial feminist writer Jill Filipovic produced what seems to me the most useful catalogue of complaints in her recent volume *OK Boomer, Let's Talk*. Filipovic gets deepest, I think, because she begins with the kind and accurate observation that, in their role as parents, boomers actually are okay. Maybe even better than okay. They "gave us a nurturing base from which to grow. They encouraged us to do what we love, pursue our passions, and never settle. They allowed us the room to explore creative fields and seek meaningful work." But, as she quickly points out, what they "did for the benefit of their own kids their generation didn't do for society at large." If they (we) insisted on finding great schooling for our kids, we didn't insist on great schools for everyone's kids: that's what Prop 13 meant. If we wanted our kids to have clean air and good food, we didn't seem to mind if other kids went without—boomers elected Reagan, whose administration insisted that ketchup counted as a vegetable. If we wanted security for ourselves, we didn't insist on it for others. Barack Obama recalled a letter he'd received while fighting for the Affordable Care Act: "She says, 'I don't want government-run health care. I don't want you meddling in the private marketplace. And keep your hands off my Medicare.'"

I use "we" in the generational sense here: I imagine many people reading this book voted against Reagan and for Obama.

In the largest sense, though, the generational critique is undeniable (that's why it stings). "On an abstract level," Gibney writes in his *Generation of Sociopaths*, "I think the worst thing they've done is destroy a sense of social solidarity, a sense of commitment to fellow citizens. That ethos is gone and it's been replaced by a cult of individualism." You can see the results in the numbers: Where the 1960s had produced the Higher Education Act, with broad support for college tuition, Reagan and Bush each made it harder to get grants, and Clinton privatized Sallie Mae, the student-loan middleman. The second Bush made it impossible to discharge student loan debts through bankruptcy (the now private Sallie Mae spent $9 million lobbying Congress to guarantee that change). So, in 1980, when I was in school, a Pell Grant covered about 70 percent of a college student's expenses at a four-year college. "By 2011," writes Filipovic, "it only covered a third." Younger people spend decades paying off debts that literally didn't exist for earlier generations, and of course the burden is magnified for Black and brown students, and for those unlucky enough to end up at for-profit colleges that specialize in "assisting" their pupils in taking out the largest possible loans. In 1998—Filipovic's numbers again—the wealth gap between young workers and those within a decade of retirement was significant: the households whose members were about to retire were worth about seven times as much as those headed by people who were twenty to thirty-five years old. That might seem reasonable, the residue of a lifetime's work. But as the various advantages of the post-Reagan ethic kept multiplying, the gap started exploding. Now, the average net worth of households headed by someone in their fifties or sixties is *twelve times* that of their younger counterparts. Actually, the average net worth of those young households *fell* by $2,600 over those decades, while the average net worth of the older cohort grew by more than $450,000. Because of those ever-appreciating suburban homes; because they had spare cash to invest. (Not because their kids were wasting money on Starbucks.) As a result, millennials are paying 40 percent more for a first home than boomers did; not surprisingly, a third of eighteen- to thirty-four-year-olds still live in a parent's home, and 20 percent have a roommate.

Or think about the carbon debt in generational terms. If you're sixty, 82 percent of the world's fossil fuel emissions have occurred in your lifetime. (For eighty-five-year-olds, the number only goes up to 90 percent, a reminder of how compressed in time the carbon explosion has been.) For three-quarters of your adult life you've known about the dangers of the climate crisis, but it hasn't impinged much if at all on your lifestyle. But now: if we're to hold the temperature increase to 1.5 degrees Celsius, as the world promised in the Paris Climate Accords, the global lifetime carbon budget for someone born today will be 43 tons of carbon dioxide, about an eighth as much as for someone born in 1950. And even if they do the hard work to meet that target, they will still get to live their lives on a planet without an Arctic, where forest fire season stretches implacably on.

All of these debts translate into, among other things, a reluctance to form families and have children. (Or, to put it another way, generational selfishness may end up costing plenty of people the grandchildren they'd been hoping for.) If you can't afford to buy a house and you're using all your money to pay off your student loans, how eager are you going to be to have kids? The average fertility rate is half what it was during the baby boom, and it may not get better. In November of 2020, researchers surveying people aged twenty-six to forty-five found that 96 percent of them were "very or extremely concerned about the wellbeing of their potential future children in a climate-changed world." One of the researchers said, "It was often heartbreaking to pore through the responses—a lot of people really poured their hearts out."

THERE ARE, IT seems to me, three ways to react to that heartbreak.

One is to pretend it doesn't exist, which is easy to do if you watch Fox News, the go-to network for older Americans (its median viewer is sixty-eight years old, which means half of them are above that). According to Fox, and to its Facebook friends, you don't need to worry much about younger generations because they're snowflakes who eat avocado toast while burning down most American cities and canceling everything that makes life worth living, such as Mr. Potato Head.

Another option is to take care of your own family and friends, and to volunteer in the community you live in to take care of some other people. All of which is fine and good, but it's sort of what got us in this mess. It's good as far as it goes, but as far as it goes isn't good enough—the wealth gap and the carbon gap keep growing.

And the third is to actually rise to the political moment and play some role in turning the clock back, or forward. Which isn't entirely far-fetched. It's true that Donald Trump carried the

senior vote in the last election, as Republicans had in every election this millennium. But his margin dropped a little. And he
was beaten by a seventy-eight-year-old man, Joe Biden, whose
political roots were very much in the pre-Reagan era. (Biden was
elected to the Senate in 1973, two years after that protest on
the Green, which was led by John Kerry, who Biden immediately named his global climate envoy.) The policies that Biden
then started pushing were far closer to, say, Lyndon Johnson's or
Hubert Humphrey's, than they were to Bill Clinton's or Barack
Obama's: his first package of COVID relief gave most families
in America a $300 monthly check for each of their kids; it was
designed to cut childhood poverty in half, and it seemed to be
working until Joe Manchin and the GOP combined to end the
experiment at the start of 2022. Then he proposed a massive
overhaul of America's infrastructure, in part designed to fight
climate change. He was able to propose these things—really he
had no choice but to try them—because the Democratic Party
had been transformed, largely by the efforts of Bernie Sanders
(now eighty) and Elizabeth Warren (seventy-two). Perhaps, in
other words, some of the generational edge in our political life
has begun to wane; perhaps we could continue to mobilize more
older people and make more progress. Perhaps not. As Ta-Nehisi
Coates pointed out in an interview in the *Times* in the summer of 2021, "There are people that I recognize I can never get
to because their imagination is already formed. And when their
imagination is formed, no amount of facts can dislodge them."

But maybe there are moments when you can teach an old dog
new tricks, or at least remind it of the tricks it learned when it
was a pup. I began this book describing a protest, and I'm going

to end it the same way, in part because I think that night on the Battle Green when I was ten did a lot to shape my sense of the world and how older people might play a part in shifting it. Remember, it was an alliance of young Vietnam veterans and older townspeople who came together that night to make change, and that's an alliance that needs rebuilding.

In the spring of 2011, I heard from Indigenous leaders about a project called Keystone XL, an eighteen-hundred-mile-long pipeline that would carry the filthy crude pumped from the tar sands of Alberta down to the Gulf of Mexico. They'd been fighting it on the—completely correct—grounds that it was wrecking their territory, and they'd been joined by farmers and ranchers in Nebraska who didn't want to give up their land. I thought it was time to see if the then small climate movement was ready to pick up its game, and so, with the blessing of the groups that had been pushing the battle, we sent the word out: come to Washington for civil disobedience outside the Obama White House in August. I wrote the letter asking people to join in, a missive signed by a passel of older activists on both sides of the border, great leaders like Tom Goldtooth of the Indigenous Environmental Network, the writer Wendell Berry, the actor and activist Danny Glover. The letter laid out the plans and then concluded with these words:

And one more thing: We don't want college-age kids to be the cannon fodder in this fight. They've led the way so far on climate change. Now it's time for people who've spent their lives pouring carbon into the atmosphere (and whose careers won't be as damaged by an arrest record) to step up too. Most of us signing this letter are veterans of this work, and we think it's past time for elders to behave like elders.

I had no idea how well the appeal would work—it had been many years since the environmental movement had tried to get people out in the street this way, and the logistics crew we were working with in Washington tempered expectations: if five or six people showed up to get arrested each day during our two-week protest, they said, that would be a lot. Still, I hoped for more.

We'd told people to come to a DC church for training, and so the night before the first protest we were waiting in the nave with some anxiety: would people respond? As it turned out, they flooded in: more than 150 for that first session alone, almost all of whom reappeared the next morning outside the White House and sat down on the sidewalk, waiting to be handcuffed. We hadn't asked people how old they were; that seemed rude. But—cleverly, I think—we did ask each person, "Who was president when you were born?" The biggest cohorts came from the FDR and Truman administrations. On the last day of the protest, the last person arrested—number 1,254, in what had turned into the biggest civil disobedience action about anything in the United States in a long time—had a sign around his neck that said, "World War II vet, Handle with Care." He was well into his nineties and had been born during the Harding administration. It was important for the young people on hand—and there were plenty—to see their elders acting the way we need elders to act.

Those of us arrested that first day were taken off to Central Cell Block in DC, which is no nicer than it sounds. We spent a few days there, and the cell next to mine housed a man named Gus Speth, who had helped found the Natural Resources Defense Council after the first Earth Day in 1970, who had then headed President Carter's Council on Environmental Quality (when those first solar panels went up) and the United Nations Development Programme and, before his retirement, the Yale School of Forestry and Environmental Studies. The ultimate insider, in other words—but who now, nearing seventy, had decided it was necessary to think very differently. He sent out a short statement to the press: "I've held many important positions in this town," he said. "But none seem as important as the one I'm in today." Watching his testimony, the heads of the country's most important environmental organizations had no real choice but to sign on: within a day they'd all joined in a letter to Obama saying, "There is not an inch of daylight between our position and those of the people getting arrested on your lawn." Within months Obama had paused the approval process for the pipeline; in his second term he rejected it altogether, saying it had failed a "climate test." It was a signal early moment in the climate fight.

In the years since, young people have transformed the climate fight, just as they have the civil rights movement. Groups like the Sunrise Movement, Fridays for Future, and Black Lives Matter, led by new generations of organizers and thinkers, have expanded and revivified these struggles, because they're able to say, quite clearly: it's we who will have to bear the results of this, our lives that will be blighted by rising temperatures and ongoing racism. And they're correct: they've earned in every sense the right to lead these battles.

But they need those of us who are older to back them up. Think about the banks that drive climate change—Chase Bank, which has loaned the fossil fuel industry a quarter trillion dollars since the Paris accords were signed, or Bank of America, or Wells Fargo, or Citi. Think about the asset managers like BlackRock or Vanguard or State Street that own the biggest chunks of oil company stock. They don't like it when young people demonstrate at their offices. But they worry more about the people whose money they hold. Between them, for the unhappy reasons I've spent this book describing, baby boomers and the silent generation control 70 percent of the nation's wealth; millennials have less than 5 percent. So mobilizing some percentage of those older Americans to sit down with their financial advisors will send a loud message back to headquarters. Boomers and the silent generation are no longer the biggest voting bloc—as of the 2020 elections, demographics had moved the younger generations into a narrow numerical lead that will only grow as funerals work their implacable change. But older Americans vote in such high percentages—74 percent in 2020, versus 57 percent of those aged eighteen to thirty-four—that we'll exert outsized power on our political system for decades to come. Shifting the attitudes of some percentage of that demographic is therefore key. And it's not just financial affluence that we have to offer, it's "time affluence": in the next twenty years, retiring boomer Americans will have 2.5 trillion leisure hours to fill. We might as well spend some of it repairing the damage we've caused; we might even enjoy the process.

We're used to the idea that people get more conservative as they age—"if you're not an idealist when you're twenty you have no heart; if you're still one at thirty you have no head," or at least no bank account. But as we live longer, that aphorism needs amending. If you're not an idealist when you're seventy or eighty you have no grandkids. We're about to be the first generation to leave the world a worse place than we found it. We're foreclosing, every day, the possibilities for our descendants. And we can overcome it only if we close the gap between—well, between the performative liberalism of that antiwar rally on Lexington Green and the private conservatism of that vote against public housing.

What happened in my suburb fifty years ago happens still. As the columnist Ezra Klein pointed out not long ago, "In much of San Francisco, you can't walk 20 feet without seeing a multi-colored sign declaring that Black lives matter, kindness is everything and no human being is illegal. Those signs sit in yards zoned for single families, in communities that organize against efforts to add the new homes that would bring those values closer to reality. Poorer families—disproportionately nonwhite and immigrant—are pushed into long commutes, overcrowded housing and homelessness." That hypocrisy prevents—in San Francisco, but in a thousand other places too—the kind of dense housing that would help ameliorate the climate crisis, just as it might help Black and brown people accumulate some wealth.

But a growing YIMBY—"yes in my backyard"—movement is beginning to shift some of that politics, and at least in some places doing it with the support not only of young people but of old. In 2019, the AARP (formerly the American Association of Retired Persons, the most effective lobbying group in the country) came out in favor of revisions to California's zoning code that would change zoning to legalize apartment buildings in many places: precisely the laws voted down in Lexington all those years

ago, precisely the laws that Nikole Hannah-Jones found enforc-
ing segregation in Westchester, precisely the laws that Donald
Trump was defending when he said, "Suburban women, will you
please like me? I saved your damn neighborhood." As one advo-
cate said: "Too many older people feel trapped in homes that
don't make sense for their lifestyles anymore, but aren't able to
scale down to an apartment in their neighborhood. It's hard to
age in place and maintain friendships in your community if it's
either maintain a suburban household or move to an assisted living facility." And, as the head of the state's AARP pointed out,
high housing costs mean people's kids can't stay in the neighborhood and help take care of them as they age. "Many older adults
who can afford to stay in California are seeing family members,
close friends, and caregivers leave the state due to the high cost
of housing," she said. "What is the point of aging in place if it
means watching everyone you love have to move away?"

But older people also have something beyond their kids and
grandkids to think about. We also have the chance to partially
redeem some sense of our history as Americans, and, for those to
whom it matters, as Christians. Conservative political leaders try
to do this by suppressing the truth—hence all those bills about
banning the teaching of the 1619 Project in our schools. In Iowa,
for instance, a bill to keep the 1619 Project, and indeed all "critical race theory," out of schools was premised on the idea that telling such truths "attempts to deny or obfuscate the fundamental
principles upon which the United States was founded." I doubt
very much whether this strategy will work: I think the actual
blood on which America was too much founded will keep seep-
ing through, staining whatever whitewash we assiduously apply. I

think the only way to make our heritage any better is to make our present and future better: if we change decisively in the direction of inclusion and fairness, then perhaps history—taking a very long view—will see something worth lauding in the promise that "all men are created equal," or in the Gospel injunction to love one's neighbor; perhaps if we install enough solar panels, then the American science and engineering of the twentieth century (which birthed those miraculous devices) will be remembered for more than making the comfortable more so.

This kind of redemption rests not on suppressing the truth of our past, but on engaging and overcoming it. It depends on us helping to usher in, instead of endlessly opposing, what Anand Giridharadas has called "a kind of society that has seldom, if ever, existed in history ... a majority-minority, democratic super-power." Redemption means actively supporting the changes required to make that transition. If, fifty years ago, people could tell themselves that the changes Dr. King and his myriad colleagues had wrought—some access to the ballot box, an end to legal segregation—were enough, we now know better. We know that it's going to take truly affirmative action to bring justice.

Some of it looks like small steps—a gentle letting go of what we now recognize as a destructive past, and its replacement with something that works for us all. Joe Biden is good at this: My favorite ad of the 2020 election featured him sitting in the front of his 1967 green Corvette Stingray, the car that his auto-dealer father had given him when he got married. "I love this car," Biden says. "Nothing but incredible memories. Every time I get in I think of my Dad and Beau. God, could my Dad drive a car. Oof." That's powerful, and powerfully fine, nostalgia: we didn't know about climate change in 1967. Muscle cars—like station wagons—were dandy. "This is an iconic industry," he continues. "How can American-made vehicles no longer be out there?" Again, reasonable nostalgia—but not the kind that moves into resentful and hopeless attempts to hold on to a different past. Instead, it's the kind of nostalgia that sees us moving forward. "I believe that we can own the twenty-first-century market again by moving to electric vehicles," Biden says. "And by the way, they tell me—and I'm looking forward, if it's true, to driving one— that they're making an electric Corvette that can go two hundred miles an hour. You think I'm kidding—I'm not kidding. So I'm excited about it." This doesn't connect with every young person in America—many of them are, rightly, looking forward to a future of working trains and buses and e-bikes. But it connects to plenty of others—it bridges from the past into a better future.

Sometimes those steps aren't so gentle or easy; they require the courage to stand up to both authority and to history. Let me describe one last protest. The same week in the summer of 2021 that Biden finally killed the Keystone XL Pipeline once and for all, many of us who'd fought that battle were up in northern Minnesota, trying to block another huge tar sands pipeline, this one called Line 3. Indigenous groups had blocked its construction through two brutal pandemic winters; now, freed by the vaccine, the rest of us could join in—and so I found myself on the banks of the headwaters of the Mississippi. Native elders were in charge of the demonstration, along with a sprinkling of other older folks, notably the actress Jane Fonda who (fifty years ago and today) has made a habit of lending her charisma to those who need it. We were staring out across a marsh at an elaborate wooden boardwalk that the pipeline company had built to take its drill rigs straight to the riverbank, and at a certain point, it became obvious what we should do next. People started to wade out across the hummocky swamp—Dawn Goodwin, an Anishinaabe woman who'd helped coordinate the protest, grabbed my hand, and soon we were sloshing through the muck, and then climbing up on top of the wooden boardwalk, which she claimed as the ancestral land it was. Soon Tom Goldtooth, veteran head of the Indigenous Environmental Network, joined us, and Nancy Beaulieu, and Winona LaDuke, and many other elders of that community. We sloshed right past the "No Trespassing" signs, and there were too many of us for the police to arrest.

As people sat on the bank of the Mississippi—so narrow here that you could hop across it—they talked about the history of treaty violations that had led to this day, and they talked too about the future: about heading off the climate chaos that comes from burning the stuff that would flow through this pipeline. I lay on that boardwalk in the hot June Minnesota sun, thinking about this most iconic of rivers and the countless chapters of American history it had witnessed: Lewis and Clark heading out from St. Louis, the slave markets of New Orleans, Dr. King, shot along its banks in Memphis. It would have been easy for the Indigenous leaders to turn away outsiders; instead, they were welcoming us. Because, practically, that's what it takes to win. And because that's what good people do: open new chapters in the human story, ones that have some hope of redeeming what came before.

NOTES, SOURCES, AND ACKNOWLEDGMENTS

I am used to writing books with extensive footnotes, but this volume is in part memoir, and so academic form seemed a little out of place; more to the point, I've come to worry that very few readers actually peruse notes, and so the authors and researchers on whom one relies receive less credit than they should. So I've tried, throughout the text, to flag the sources I was relying on, in hopes others would seek them out. I'll repeat that exercise a little more formally here, interspersed with acknowledgments to others who helped in various ways to make this book possible.

The book opens with a short history of Lexington in the postwar years, leading to two crucial events—mass arrests on the Battle Green as part of a protest against the war in Vietnam, and a referendum on affordable housing. Let me begin, then, by thanking the two people to whom this book is dedicated. If my parents had not moved to Lexington—inspired in part, I think, by the promise of its excellent schools for me and my brother—this story would not exist. More pointedly, though, if they hadn't taken us down to the Green to watch those protests unfold, and if my father had not decided to get himself arrested, and if my mother had not been willing to take us home to bed so that would be possible—well, certainly this book would not have been written, but I'm also not at all sure I would have led the life that I've lived, a life informed by dissent.

My account of the town's history is informed by the work of Richard Kollen, particularly his book *From Liberty's Birthplace to Progressive Suburb.* I also leaned heavily on a slim book published by Alice Hinkle and Andrea Cleghorn, *Life in Lexington, 1946–1995.* In 1992 a local resident named Eugenia Kaledin gathered many neighbors to create the Lexington Oral History Project, a series of interviews with people involved in the 1971 protests in the Battle Green. Their efforts—easily available online, and through the Open Archive project of the University of Massachusetts Boston—were of tremendous value to me. And I need to acknowledge an even larger debt here. I relied heavily on the coverage of these events in the pages of the *Lexington Minuteman* (the crucial years for this book, conveniently, have been digitized and are available through the website of Lexington's superb Cary Memorial Library). But the *Minuteman* was also the place where, beginning at age fourteen, I started learning the craft of journalism, covering soccer and basketball at 25 cents the column inch, and where I soon was spending my summers writing news and features. Anne Scigliano, my first boss, is quoted in these pages because she was running the paper at the time of these events; her successor, Mike Rosenberg, taught me a great deal about newspapering when I was in my high school years. The *Minuteman* was the prototype of a local newspaper, offering in-depth coverage of a town of thirty thousand in a fashion that has largely disappeared. I also used back issues of the Lexington High School *Musket*—and my co-editor of that newspaper, Jon Miller, provided a truly useful early reading of the drafts of this book. Census data came in handy throughout, and Harvard's Jill Lepore provided useful advice about how to make use of it.

The first section of this book, "The Flag," relies a great deal on histories of the American Revolution, both the traditional sources and the powerful revisions of recent years. Richard John, with whom I guided tourists on the Battle Green as a teenager, helped point me in useful directions. I have always been inspired by Gordon Wood's arguments in his *The Radicalism of the American Revolution*. George Daughan's 2018 volume *Lexington and Concord: The Battle Heard Round the World* is a useful collation of the latest scholarship on the first fight of that war; the same for Rick Atkinson's *The British Are Coming*. Robert Gross, in *The Minutemen and Their World*, provides a vivid picture of life in Middlesex County in the 1770s. But our understanding, both of Lexington and of the Revolution, has of course been helpfully if painfully complicated in recent years by the essential work of historians focused on the unglorious parts of the story. Nikole Hannah-Jones and her colleagues on the 1619 Project deserve every accolade they've received, and far more: it's fair, I think, to say that no single work of history has done more to recalibrate and reorient our understanding of the past (including inspiring many local historiographers, who will deepen and enrich this account in the years to come). In Lexington, Alice

Hinkle worked diligently to uncover what we can recover of the story of Prince Estabrook, the lone enslaved person who was present on the Green. Margot Minardi, in her *Making Slavery History: Abolitionism and the Politics of Memory in Massachusetts*, provides invaluable background on the depth and persistence of slavery and racism in Massachusetts. The unbearable history of Mark Codman and his sister Phillis has been told less fully than it should—there are glimpses of the story in journalist Francie Latour's account for the *Boston Globe*, "New England's Hidden History," and an 1883 account of the trial by Abner Cheney Goodell can be found online thanks to Project Gutenberg.

Woody Holton, in his book *Forced Founders: Indians, Debtors, Slaves, and the Making of the American Revolution in Virginia*; David Waldstreicher, in *Runaway America: Benjamin Franklin, Slavery, and the American Revolution*; and Mary V. Thompson, in her *"The Only Unavoidable Subject of Regret": George Washington, Slavery, and the Enslaved Community at Mount Vernon*, helped me see figures that were part of my mental furniture in new and useful lights. David McCullough's *The Pioneers: The Heroic Story of the Settlers Who Brought the American Ideal West* is far more traditional, but his book was very useful to me because it concentrated on the territory along the Ohio River where my mother came of age; it wasn't very hard to read between the lines and figure out the less-than-heroic parts of the story, especially as they related to the treatment of Native Americans. I am sorry to merely brush by that bleak part of American history in this book.

As I tried to talk about the story of race in Lexington in my time, I was grateful for a few documents, especially Mike Mascoll's film accounts in *On the Line* and *CodeSwitching*. Matthew

Resseger's work on housing in Massachusetts was extremely helpful, including his Harvard doctoral thesis. And in a larger vein, Nikole Hannah-Jones's work for ProPublica on housing policy (which preceded the 1619 Project and her employment at the *Times*) was crucial. Her reporting on the federal failure to integrate Westchester County is among the finest pieces of modern investigative journalism (and would, by itself, make a mockery of the absurd decision of the University of North Carolina not to grant her tenure as a journalism professor). As the discussion moves to reparations, I am of course simply following the lead of Ta-Nehisi Coates, whose work on the subject has been the most telling magazine journalism of our time; if you somehow haven't read his books, you should probably put this one down and start there. Many thanks as well to Richard Rothstein for his epic *The Color of Law,* which helped transform my understanding of housing discrimination and allied issues. I've also learned a lot from reading Nkechi Taifa.

The second main section of this book, "The Cross," begins with some descriptions of the church I grew up in, the Hancock United Church of Christ. (Richard Kollen provided useful accounts of its predecessor congregations.) I'm very grateful to the women and men who taught me there, beginning with Jackie Childs; Ed McLane oversaw my confirmation class, and his kindness stays with me. I'm also very indebted to some of their successors, particularly Dan Smith, who I quote extensively, and to the current pastors and staff who, among other things, continue to make my mother a full part of church life. There is much less good writing on the quotidian life of American Christianity in our time than there should be—and an enormous percentage of it comes from the generous and incisive mind of Diana Butler Bass. Her long bibliography was of great value to my research; her newsletter *The Cottage* of great value to my ongoing life. Jemar Tisby, with his book *The Color of Compromise: The Truth About the American Church's Complicity in Racism*, has greatly advanced our understanding; the same is true for Robert P. Jones and his *White Too Long: The Legacy of White Supremacy in American Christianity*, and Kristin Kobes Du Mez, in her *Jesus and John Wayne: How White Evangelicals Corrupted a Faith and Fractured a Nation*.

Many thanks to James Hudnut-Beumler and Mark Silk for their magisterial *The Future of Mainline Protestantism in America;* to Jim Wallis and *Sojourners* magazine, where I've written a regular column for many years; and to Mark Labberton for editing the collection of essays *Still Evangelical? Insiders Reconsider Political, Social, and Theological Meaning*. A great deal of my thinking on these questions traces back to the late Rev. Peter Gomes; if I could persuade people to read a single book about Christianity, it would be his *The Scandalous Gospel of Jesus: What's So Good About the Good News?*

The final large section of this book, "The Station Wagon," draws on many of the same sources I've already mentioned for its close reading of prosperity in Lexington in particular and the suburbs in general. (And man, Zillow comes in handy too.) Meg Jacobs, in her *Panic at the Pump: The Energy Crisis and the Transformation of American Politics in the 1970s,* was very helpful in reconstructing the politics of the era. I'm also struck, looking back at the end of the Carter years and the beginning of the Reagan era, with how much I owe my colleagues first at the *Harvard*

Crimson and second at the *New Yorker*, where I arrived in 1982. In particular, hardly a day passed for the five years I spent on West Forty-Third Street without a long conversation with Jonathan Schell; Mr. Shawn, somewhat improbably, let a twenty-one-year-old opine regularly in his Comment section. (And of course I'm deeply grateful to David Remnick for restoring the *New Yorker* in recent decades; I've found a happy home there, mulling over much that is contained in these pages; my regular editor Virginia Cannon could not have been more helpful.)

This book closes with a few reflections on who should be taking up the fight to repair the damage chronicled in its pages. I vote for the boomers and the silent generation above them; having caused many of the problems, we have the resources and the skills to back up younger generations as they try to make repairs. I've tried to credit some of the writers who have written lucidly about generational conflict, especially Helen Andrews and Jill Filipovic. But I'm mostly grateful for those who are helping build Third Act, the movement that has occupied much of my time in recent years. Vanessa Arcara has been at the forefront of this effort, and she has also been the glue that held together my professional life as I was writing this book; many thanks on similar grounds to Veronique Graham, and to Third Act's leader Akaya Windwood, and its early staff, including Bob Fulkerson, Anna Goldstein, Hypatia Sorunke, and Deborah Moore.

As always—from my very first book—I have relied on my agent, Gloria Loomis. I am happy to still be at Holt, with a fine new editor in Sarah Crichton and her assistant, Natalia Ruiz, with dear longtime colleagues in the publicity department and, especially, associate publisher Maggie Richards. The remarkable editorial freedom at Substack, where I publish a newsletter called *The Crucial Years*, has let me try out ideas easily. And of course none of my work would be possible without my home base at Middlebury College, with its fearless leader, Laurie Patton.

And, far more, without my home base at home, with *its* fearless leader, Sue Halpern, and her sidekick, Birke the dog. I've come a long ways from that boyhood in Lexington, and I've been lucky to arrive at a very good place.

ABOUT THE AUTHOR

BILL MCKIBBEN is a founder of the environmental organization 350.org and was among the first to have warned of the dangers of global warming. He is the author of more than a dozen books, including the best sellers *The End of Nature*, *Eaarth*, and *Deep Economy*.

He is the Schumann Distinguished Scholar in Environmental Studies at Middlebury College and the winner of the Gandhi Peace Award, the Thomas Merton Award, and the Right Livelihood Award, sometimes called "the alternate Nobel." He lives in Vermont with his wife, the writer Sue Halpern. His new project, organizing people over sixty for progressive change, is called Third Act.